DREAM JOURNEYS

068 365 973

DREAM JOURNEYS

THE WORLD'S MOST UNFORGETTABLE JOURNEYS

MARY-ANN GALLAGHER

Quercus

CONTENTS

8 The Pan-American Highway

16 The Alaskan Coast

34 Parc National du Bic to Carleton

12 Route 66

24 The Rockies by train

28 The Appalachian Trail

20 The Pacific Coast Highway

30 The Yucatán Peninsula

40 The Caribbean islands

48 El Chepe

36 Costa Rica

44 The Amazon

50 The Inca Trail

54 To the ends of the world

100 The Golden Circle

58 The Orient Express

84 The Sky Road

66 The Norwegian Coast

96 The Weser Renaissance Route

104 The Castle Road

74 The Romantic Road

112 The Italian Lakes

124 The Trans-Siberian Express

92 The Grandes Alpes Route

108 The Dalmatian Coast

120 The Silk Route

78 The Corniches

116 The Amalfi Coast

82 The Spine of Corsica

136 The Kii Peninsu

70 The Trans-Pyrenean Route

128 The Ganges

62 El Camino de Santiago

164 The Golden Triangle

88 Andalucía's white villages

132 The Grand Trunk Road

152 The High Atlas Mountains

148 Sailing down the Nile

186 The Saigon-Hanoi Express

146 Mount Kilimanjaro

188 The Headhunter Trail

156 Along the Skeleton Coast

142 The African Lakes

172 Cape York

168 A Tropical paradise

160 The Okavango Delta

174 The Great Ocean Road

138 The Garden Route

178 North Island

182 The Milford Track

INTRODUCTION

This book covers 50 inspirational journeys across the globe, taking you from the very ends of the Earth in Antarctica to the highest peaks of great mountains such as Kilimanjaro. These journeys are made on foot, by boat, by car, by train and by plane, traversing jungles and deserts, magnificent cities and some of the most remote terrain in the world. Glide through remote Amazonian forest in dug-out canoes, island-hop across Indonesia or the Caribbean, or soar above the roaring dunes of Namibia's Skeleton Coast.

Many of these journeys will take you back in time, following in the footsteps of the Incas who built the great temple complex of Machu Picchu in the 15th century, or the traders who crossed Asia with their caravans of silk and spices along the Silk Road almost 2,000 years ago. We explore the enchanting medieval towns of Germany and the Czech Republic, many still crowned by fairytale castles, and the glittering temples of the Lanna kingdom, which once ruled much of northern Thailand. In Iceland, a jagged rock rising from a scarred, craggy plain still marks the site of the first ever European parliament, the Althing, which first gathered there in 930 AD. In the northern tip of Australia, Aboriginal rock art dating back tens of thousands of years still gleams in remote caves, and, along the shores of the mighty River Nile, temples built by the ancient Egyptians still stand sentinel after several millennia. In the heart of Andalucía in Spain, we explore the front line of the Reconquista, where Christian armies from the north battled with the Muslim Moors to regain the peninsula during the 13th and 14th centuries. The dazzling whitewashed villages betray their Arabic origins with twisting narrow streets, and sturdy medieval fortresses stud the hills. Our Alaskan journey reveals an intriguing mixture of cultures, from the indigenous peoples that have occupied the frozen lands for millennia to the Russians, Norwegians and other Europeans who arrived in the 18th and 19th centuries seeking gold and trade. In Samarkand, glittering madrasas and mausolea recall the glory of Timur, who ruled a vast empire in Central Asia. We also dip into more recent history, slipping back to the golden age of train travel with a journey on the Orient Express, which boasts sumptuously refurbished carriages from the 1920s and '30s. Historic Route 66, spanning the USA from Chicago to Los Angeles, evokes the freedom and romance of one of the world's great road journeys, with its streamlined Art Deco motels, diners and gas stations.

We follow ancient pilgrimage routes, such as the Camino de Santiago, which culminates in the glorious city of Santiago de Compostela, where the bones of Saint James are kept within a magnificent cathedral. Deep in the remote forests of Japan's Kii Peninsula, we visit temples and shrines built by powerful emperors a thousand years ago, and in Indonesia we make our path to the largest Buddhist shrine on earth, a vast temple-pyramid erected in 750 AD as a physical representation of Buddhist cosmology. In Central America, spectacular stepped temples stand as testament to the Mayan civilization's grasp of astronomy, mathematics and construction techniques. Built without the aid of metal tools, work animals or even the wheel, these extraordinary edifices continue to inspire awe and wonder. A journey through India follows the sacred River Ganges, revered by Hindus as the embodiment of the great goddess Ganga. Several pilgrimage sites have grown up on her banks, including magnificent Varanasi, the holiest city in the Hindu world. To die in Varanasi is to attain *moksha* – a release from the endless cycle of reincarnation, and a direct passage to nirvana.

Our journeys take us through the world's spectacular natural wonders, from sweltering jungle to frozen islands, and from explosive volcanoes to dramatic fjords. We visit the world's largest river, the largest waterfall, the largest freestanding mountain, and the world's oldest geyser (Great Geyser, in Iceland). The Okavango in Botswana is the only river in the world to culminate in desert, splitting into an infinite mesh of streams and rivulets that attract an astonishing variety of wildlife, including lion, elephant, zebra, wildebeest, giraffe, gazelle, hippopotamus, crocodile and rhino. We range through the immense rainforest of the Amazon, which shelters more species of plant and animal life than anywhere else on Earth, and explore remote tributaries by riverboat and canoe. Costa Rica, one of the world's most ecologically diverse nations, boasts pristine cloud forest, fuming volcanoes and glorious white-sand beaches where turtles come to breed on moonlit nights. Approximately a quarter of the country is protected in conservation areas, which support more than 500,000 species of flora and fauna, among them jaguars, ocelots, tapirs and butterflies as well as more than 400 species of bird, such as the elusive quetzal, famous for its brilliant coloured plumage. The Indonesian island of Sumatra, swathed in dense forest, is home to several endangered species, including the Sumatran Tiger, the Sumatran Orangutan and the Sumatran rhino. At the southern tip of Indonesia, New Guinea's extraordinary coastline is rimmed with coral reefs, attracting a dazzling array of marine creatures. New Zealand's spectacular scenery ranges from the mirror-like lakes and jagged inlets of the Fiordland National Park, to the sacred peak of Tongariro crowned by an electric-blue lake. Iceland is a geological hotspot, a land of fire and ice, and its surreal, volcanic landscape is pocked by steaming mud pools and explosive geysers. Down in the frozen wastes of Antarctica, enormous colonies of penguins congregate on the shores of islands too remote and inhospitable to sustain human life, although whales, sea lions, elephant seals and orca whales abound. Much of the Garden Route, along South Africa's most verdant coastline, is protected by a vast national park, a magnificent wilderness encompassing limpid lakes and lagoons, wave-lashed headlands and dense forest.

Among our journeys are some of the world's most thrilling hikes. These include the celebrated Inca trail high in the Andes, and the headhunters' trail in Borneo, which follows the ancient warring routes of remote island tribes. We clamber among the pristine forests and scenic peaks of the Appalachians in the United States, and plunge into the sacred mountains of southern Japan. We trek across the spine of Corsica and along the heady peaks of Morocco's High Atlas, ascend the steep slopes of Kilimanjaro, and span the length of the Spanish Pyrenees, from the Mediterreanean Sea to the Atlantic Ocean.

The thrill of the road is encapsulated in iconic drives such as the Pan-American Highway, the world's longest thoroughfare, which stretches from Alaska to the very tip of Argentina, and the Grand Trunk Road, which sweeps from the Afghan border across Pakistan and northern India. The narrow, cliff-hugging road that curves around the Amalfi Coast melds the natural splendour of rugged peaks with picture-postcard images of medieval villages spilling down into an azure sea. There are more hairpin bends and breathtaking bays along the legendary Pacific Coast Highway, which weaves its way from San Diego to the redwood forests of California. Back in Europe, we take a spin around the Italian Lakes, set against a dazzling Alpine backdrop, the villas and gardens recalling the aristocratic age of the Grand Tour at the turn of the 19th century. Ireland's captivating Sky Road meanders around a ravishing peninsula, etched with little bays and tiny hamlets, with Connemara ponies grazing in the meadows, and seals bobbing off the coast. We tackle off-road terrain in the northern tip of Australia, penetrating the unspoilt wilderness of Cape York.

We've included some extraordinary train journeys, from the grande luxe of the Orient Express to the considerably simpler yet no less atmospheric accommodations of the great Trans-Siberian Express, which chugs across the Siberian steppes on its seven-day journey from Moscow to Vladivostock, crossing two continents and seven time zones. The 'El Chepe' train winds across Mexico's Sierra Madre mountain range, scored with deep gorges and scattered with remote villages and waterfalls. Cross the Canadian Rockies, capped with snow and swathed in forest, in the Rocky Mountaineer, a lavishly appointed tourist train that follows the historic route of the trans-continental Canadian railway.

And then there are the boat journeys, from a languid cruise up the Nile in a white-sailed felucca, to an island-hop around the dazzling blue waters of the Caribbean, or the tropical seas in Indonesia. We dawdle in the unspoilt islands off the Dalmatian Coast in Croatia, and paddle in dug-out canoes through the game-rich wetlands of the Okavango Delta.

Mary-Ann Gallagher

The Pan-American Highway begins in the far north of Alaska and makes its way south through Canada's spectacular Yukon Territory, shown here. On its long route, the highway crosses many diverse climates, from high mountain passes to dense jungles and arid deserts. Some stretches of the highway are passable only during the dry season.

Start Prudhoe Bay **End** Ushuaia

Countries crossed Canada, USA, Mexico, Guatemala, El Salvador, Honduras, Nicaragua, Costa Rica, Panama, Colombia, Ecuador, Peru, Chile, Argentina

Distance 48,000 kilometres (29,800 miles)

Transport used Car, ferry

Highlights Alaska Highway, Panama Canal, Darién Gap, Andean Mountains

THE PAN-AMERICAN HIGHWAY

The Pan-American Highway crosses 14 nations, covers thousands of kilometres, and is considered the world's longest thoroughfare. It is not a single entity, but rather an enormous road network that runs the entire length of the Americas. Crossing the Americas from point to point remains the ultimate challenge for many motorists.

The Alaskan portion of the Pan-American Highway begins at Prudhoe Bay, a minuscule hamlet by the Arctic Ocean. Just south of Fairbanks, it becomes the Alaska Highway (also known as the 'Alcan' for Alaska-Canada), a spectacular drive fringed in parts with creeping glaciers. Despite the name, this is still a two-lane road for most of its length, and the permafrost means that the road surface is generally poor. It is not unusual for wildlife, including bear, moose and caribou, to wander onto the road. The scenery – dense forests and turquoise lakes – is unspoilt.

The Alaska Highway extends through the Yukon, then ends at Dawson Creek in British Columbia. From here to the Mexican border, the Pan-American Highway is not officially defined. The most common route is to travel south through Edmonton and cross into the United States near Billings, Montana. The interstate highways slice through the USA to cross the border into Mexico just beyond Laredo, Texas.

Mexico built and financed its own section of the Pan-American Highway, which is also signposted as the Inter-American Highway or the Federal Highway 85.

The dense forest of the Darién Gap is home to the gentle and slow-moving three-toed sloth. This gap in the Pan-American Highway is only 160 kilometres (100 miles) long, but it spans a wide variety of terrain, from mountainous rainforest on the northern Panama section to flat, sprawling marshland on the southern Colombian side formed by the delta of the Atrato River.

It is a wide, well-maintained road that curves through the Sierra Madre Oriental mountains before arriving in Mexico City, the country's sprawling, anarchic capital.

Federal Highway 190 runs south of Mexico City through the state of Oaxaca, home to 16 officially recognized indigenous peoples. At Ciudad Cuauhtémoc, the Mexican section of the Pan-American Highway ends, to be renamed the Central American Highway 1 as it crosses the border into Guatemala. Guatemala City, the nation's capital, has a clutch of fine monuments, including the remains of the Mayan city of Kaminaljuyu. Heading into El Salvador, the route passes the capital of San Salvador at the foot of the Quetzaltepec volcano. It skims the corner of Honduras before it plunges on into Nicaragua, where you can stop at the enormous Lake Nicaragua, or spend a few nights on a Pacific beach. The route follows the coastline of Costa Rica before cutting inland to the capital San José then continuing south to Panama.

Crossing the Centennial Bridge, the latest bridge to span the Panama Canal, the Pan-American Highway continues into sprawling, exuberant, multi-cultural Panama City. But only a few kilometres beyond the city, the highway peters out, overwhelmed by the jungle at the little town of Yaviza. This marks the beginning of the Darién Gap, where forests and swamps have combined to form a dense wilderness that has become a refuge for drug traffickers and guerrilla armies. The Darién Gap occupies the slim strip of land that links Central and South America. Travellers have no option but to take a ferry to the port of Buenaventura in Colombia.

From Colombia, the Pan-American Highway ascends into the eastern slopes of the Andes before reaching the border with Ecuador at Pasto. The road is mountainous and often poorly kept as it unfurls through Ecuador, but it links several of its major cities, including the capital Quito and the beautiful UNESCO-listed city of Cuenca. Journeying south into Peru, it hugs the coast, passing the semi-tropical beaches of Tumbes and Piura, and continuing on to the enormous capital city of Lima. In Chile, the route follows Highway 5, passing through luxuriant forest and hills on its way to Santiago. The road crosses into Argentina through a tunnel burrowed through the Andes, and then strikes south towards the glamorous capital of Buenos Aires. The final stretch follows the Atlantic coast to its culmination at Ushuaia, in the Tierra del Fuego region, which feels like it is at the very end of the world.

ROUTE 66

Start Chicago **End** Los Angeles

Countries crossed USA **Distance** 3,940 kilometres (2,448 miles) **Transport used** Car

Highlights Classic motels, diners, billboards and roadside attractions, Meteor Crater, Painted Desert and Petrified Forest National Park, Los Angeles

Nowhere evokes the romance of the open road quite like Route 66, which linked Chicago to Los Angeles for almost six decades. America's first paved highway crossed eight states and three time zones on its 3,940-kilometre (2,448-mile)-long journey to California. Eulogized by John Steinbeck, Jack Kerouac and Bob Dylan, it encapsulates the history of 20th-century America. For Depression-era migrants heading west to seek their fortunes it was the 'Mother Road', and for the Beat generation of the 1950s it was the 'Main Street of America', packed with thrills and excitement. After two decades of decline, Route 66 was finally decommissioned in 1985, superseded by multi-lane interstates. However, historic sections of the road have recently been revived. It may not be possible to drive Route 66 uninterrupted all the way from Chicago to Los Angeles, but enough preserved sections survive to relive this iconic highway's golden age. On its long journey across the United States, Route 66 takes in cosmopolitan cities, rural villages, farmland and deserts.

Driving Route 66 is an exhilarating experience for the sheer nostalgic delight evoked by the classic motels, diners and roadside attractions established in its heyday. For the first two decades of the Route's existence, it was inextricably linked with the great exodus from Oklahoma, when thousands of 'Okies' headed west to escape the hopeless poverty of the dustbowl. The optimism of the years following the end of the Depression changed the character of the road dramatically. No longer merely an escape route, it became a destination in its own right. This coincided with an explosion in car ownership.

The original Route 66 has seen a major revival recently. In 1985, the route was removed from the official United States Highway System, but portions of the route, such as this one in California, have been redesignated 'State Route 66'. Other sections are found on maps as 'Historic Route 66'.

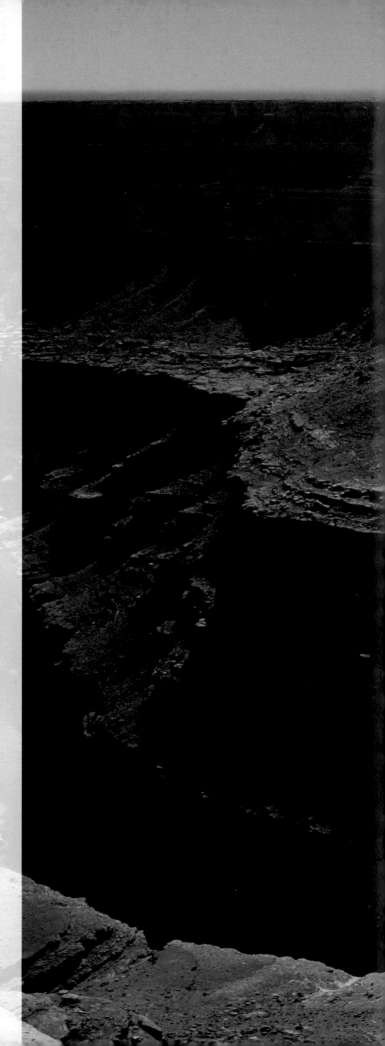

Just a few minutes' detour from Route 66 takes you to the breathtaking Grand Canyon, Arizona. More than 1,600 metres (1 mile) deep at its lowest point, the canyon was formed from 2 billion years of erosion by the Colorado River and its tributaries.

As newly affluent Americans began to travel, motels, service stations and restaurants sprang up. Some still survive, including such surreal curiosities as the Wigwam motels in San Bernadino, California, and Holbrook, Arizona, and the three 'Illinois Brothers' – gigantic statues of bearded men who enticed drivers into auto-repair shops in the 1950s. In the 1960s and '70s, ever-wilder attractions were added, such as the Blue Whale at Catoosa, which guarded a popular swimming hole for road-weary travellers and is now a picnic spot. Several landmark eateries still survive, including Lou Mitchell's diner in Chicago, nicknamed 'the first stop on the Mother Road', and the Big Texan Steak Ranch, which offers free 2-kilo (72-oz) steaks to anyone who can eat them in under an hour.

Although much of Route 66 was abandoned during the 1980s, it has seen a marked revival in its fortunes in the last decade or so. Each of the eight states associated with the route has museums dedicated to it, including one in the former Standard Oil Gasoline Station in Odell, Illinois, a whitewashed structure built in the 1930s. Some states have kept the old '66' designation on parts of the highway. Arizona preserves the longest surviving section of the original route, particularly around Flagstaff, a popular destination since the 1930s due to its proximity to the Grand Canyon.

The Grand Canyon is just one of the remarkable destinations that can be visited with a short detour from Route 66. Others include the Meteor Crater near Diabolo, a gigantic hole blasted into the Arizona desert about 50,000 years ago; the desert city of Las Vegas, world-renowned for its casinos, luxury hotels and outrageous architecture; and the glossy cinematic capital of Los Angeles at its western terminus. In Arizona, the route sweeps through the Painted Desert and Petrified Forest National Park, a remarkable blood-red landscape that richly rewards a few days' exploration.

TRAVELLER'S **TIPS**

Best time to go: Route 66 is best in spring and autumn; cold winters in the north and burning summers in the south can make for uncomfortable driving.

Look out for: There are several possible side trips off Route 66, of which the most famous are to Las Vegas and the Grand Canyon.

Dos and don'ts: Do make sure you pick up specialist maps in advance, as Route 66 is not marked on current standard maps.

THE ALASKAN COAST

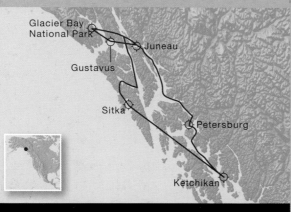

Glacier Bay National Park
Juneau
Gustavus
Sitka
Petersburg
Ketchikan

Start Juneau **End** Juneau

Countries crossed USA

Distance 970 kilometres (600 miles) **Transport used** Ferry and plane

Highlights Juneau, Glacier Bay, Sitka, Ketchikan, Misty Fjords, Petersburg

This journey makes a loop around Alaska's Inside Passage, a magnificent waterway carved by glaciers into fjords, islands and bays thousands of years ago. Its snowcapped mountains, islands, rivers and coves are justly celebrated for their pristine beauty and abundant wildlife. The region is sparsely populated, but its small communities display a unique fusion of cultures bequeathed by the native tribes, who have occupied these lands for millennia, with those of the Russians and North Americans who came in search of gold during the 19th century.

Juneau, the capital of Alaska, a lively harbour city hugged by ice-capped mountains and glaciers, has become the main cruise-ship and ferry terminal for the Inside Passage. The area has been inhabited for thousands of years by the Tlingit, Haida and Tsimshian peoples, but its modern history begins in the 1890s with the Alaskan Gold Rush. In downtown Juneau, the famous Alaskan seafood is available at numerous waterfront restaurants. The vast Juneau ice-fields stretch for more than 4,000 square kilometres (1,500 sq miles) behind the city, offering incomparable opportunities for a glacier trek.

If the weather is fine, bird's-eye vistas over the rippling peaks and forested bays await on the 20-minute flight across the Inside Passage from Juneau to Gustavus. This village is the main gateway to Glacier Bay National Park, the world's largest protected water area park. It is ringed by mountains, and glaciers slip into the limpid waters, while the craggy coastline is pocked by fjords and waterfalls. Explore the secret coves and inlets by sea kayak for glimpses of the brown and black bear or the endangered sea otter, or take a cruise through Glacier Bay for the majestic sight of glaciers calving.

The most popular and rewarding activity in Glacier Bay is whale-watching: humpbacks, orcas, minke and grey whales are just some of the species that gather to feed between June and September before making their journey south for the winter.

Great boulders of broken glacier wash ashore at Muir Inlet in the Glacier Bay National Park, creating a 'garden' of ice, beautiful in the evening light.

This Tlingit totem pole stands in the Saxman Totem Park in Ketchikan. Carved from the trunks of tall cedar trees, totem poles recount familiar stories, mark significant events or are simply made as artistic pieces. The traditional skills needed to carve the poles are kept alive with the help of commissions from parks and wealthy individuals. One totem pole may take a year to complete.

Return to Juneau, and take the ferry south for a spectacular day-long journey along the Inside Passage to Sitka, which was the capital of Russian Alaska until the Americans purchased the region in 1867. The onion domes of its Russian Orthodox cathedral still float above the little town, which sits on an island-flecked bay ringed by snow-capped mountains. After years of fighting, the Russians finally took the indigenous Tlingit fort in a bloody battle in 1804, an event remembered in the Sitka National Historic Park, where a clearing stands as a reminder of the destroyed fort. The surrounding forest is now full of hiking trails, and displays a superb collection of carved totem poles donated by several of the indigenous tribes of Alaska, including the Tlingits and the Haida. Just outside the park, the renovated 19th-century Bishop's House is one of very few surviving examples of Russian colonial architecture in the western hemisphere. Sitka also offers a host of activities, including hikes up the volcano Mount Edgecumbe, fishing, diving, kayaking and bird-watching (the neighbouring island of St Lazaria is a bird sanctuary). Sitka sits on the western coast of Baronof Island, one of three major islands covered by the enormous Tongass National Forest, the largest contiguous temperate rainforest in the world. Its remote, verdant peaks protect the rare Alaskan bear and bald eagle.

A 40-minute flight south of Sitka will bring you to Ketchikan, one of the largest towns on the Inside Passage, with a busy harbour full of ferries and floatplanes, and a thriving fishing industry. The salmon-rich rivers brought the first Tlingits to the region, and fishing remains one of the area's biggest attractions. It also boasts the world's largest collection of standing totem poles, displayed in the Totem Bight State Park, the Totem Heritage Center and in the Saxman Native Village. Behind the city, excellent walking trails extend up the slopes of Deer Mountain. The greatest highlight of the Ketchikan area is undoubtedly Misty Fjords National Monument, which is accessible only by boat, kayak or floatplane. Here, you find a spellbinding landscape of sheer volcanic cliffs, limpid waters and rushing waterfalls.

On the ferry north to Juneau, stop at Petersburg, founded by Scandinavian settlers in the late 19th century and still sometimes known as 'Little Norway'. The gigantic cruise ships can't negotiate its narrow channel, and the town has preserved its authentic atmosphere, complete with wooden boardwalks and colourfully painted façades that use a Norwegian technique called rosemaling. From Petersburg, you can choose to fly or take the ferry back to Juneau.

A magnificent 30-tonne humpback whale breaches in the Inside Passage. Whales can be seen in Alaska from early spring, when grey whales pass through on their annual migration to the Arctic Ocean. Humpbacks, killer whales and minke can be spotted throughout the brief Alaskan summer.

TRAVELLER'S **TIPS**

Best time to go: Visit from late April to early September. May is the driest month. The salmon leap is from July to September, whale-watching best from June to September.

Look out for: Specialist tour operators can arrange activities such as glacier-hiking, fishing, kayaking and wildlife-watching. Many can be booked online in advance.

Dos and don'ts: Do be prepared for severe weather, as conditions can change abruptly. Do book flights well in advance, as they fill up quickly in summer.

When it was completed in 1932, the Bixby Creek Bridge, located some 21 kilometres (13 miles) south of Carmel, allowed cars to reach the remote coastal settlements, such as Big Sur, for the first time.

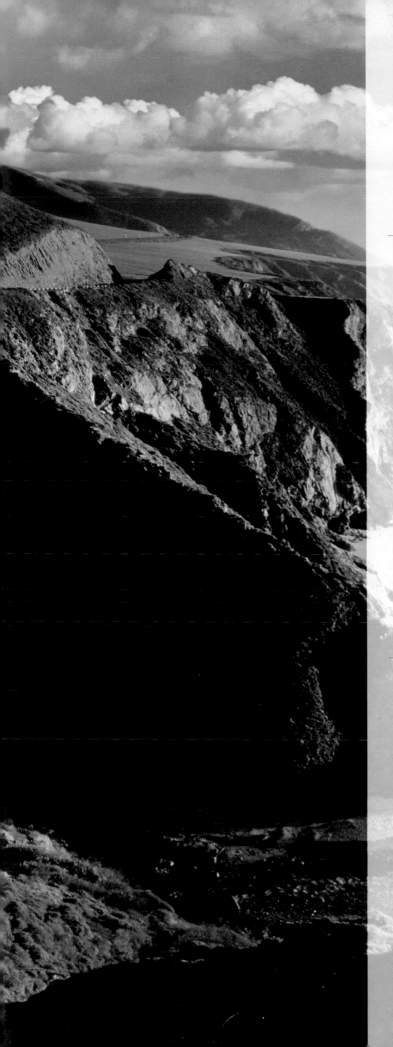

THE PACIFIC COAST HIGHWAY

Humboldt
Redwoods
State Park

San Francisco

Santa Cruz

Santa Barbara

Los Angeles

San Diego

Start San Diego
End Humboldt Redwoods State Park

Countries crossed USA

Distance 1,115 kilometres (718 miles)

Transport used Car

Highlights Wild coastline, whale-watching, Venice Beach, Hearst Castle, Carmel

One of the world's greatest road trips, the Californian stretch of the Pacific Coast Highway encompasses glorious cliffs and secret bays, the bright lights and glitter of Los Angeles and San Francisco, and the old world charm of artist enclaves such as Carmel and Mondecino. This route begins in the laid-back city of San Diego on the Mexican border and ends in the mighty redwood forests of northern California.

San Diego contains a cluster of historic buildings with the 18th-century Spanish-built Mission at its heart. But its greatest attractions are its beaches, the zoo and the Seaworld water park. From there, the highway heads north past the trendy enclave of La Jolla, where seals loll on the rocks, towards the Torrey Pines State Natural Reserve. This wild and empty stretch of coastline is blanketed in pine forest, and myriad waterbirds congregate on the silvery lagoon. Continue north to reach the relaxed communities of Laguna Beach and Newport Beach, while a short detour inland reaches Los Angeles itself.

Travelling north, the highway hugs the coast, passing Venice Beach, with its colourful murals and relaxed, boho vibe, before reaching Malibu, where movie stars and millionaires live behind gates in their rarely glimpsed mansions. Malibu's breathtaking beaches are popular with surfers. Santa Barbara, farther north, is beautifully set against the Santa Ynez mountains, which drop down to the sea, where more golden beaches extend for miles. Named after an 18th-century Spanish Mission, Santa Barbara was rebuilt in the Spanish Colonial Revival style after it was razed by an earthquake in 1925, giving the city a distinctly Mediterranean feel.

21

The bright lights of the funfair on the Santa Monica pier flicker in the waters of the Pacific. Santa Monica, which lies in western Los Angeles, has long sandy beaches and an agreeable climate, making it a popular tourist destination.

The road sweeps north of Santa Barbara, passing through low-key beach towns like Pismo Beach and Morro Bay, where a rocky islet in the middle of the bay is home to peregrine falcons. Beyond Morro Bay, the cliffs are taller and the scenery wilder. The highway hugs the forested slopes of the Santa Lucia mountains, which drop precipitously into the crashing surf below. Just beyond San Simeon, the Hearst Castle estate is a fantastical Mediterranean Revival castle filled with artworks and surrounded by gardens. Farther north, the artsy community of Big Sur is home to the Esalen Institute, where travellers can bathe in natural hot springs on the cliff top. The road then drops down to Monterey Bay, passing through the delightful artists' colony of Carmel and reaching Monterey with its famous aquarium.

The next community on this stretch of coast is Santa Cruz, which boasts a wonderful turn-of-the-20th-century boardwalk, complete with historic funfair. The highway follows the curve of the San Francisco Peninsula before arriving in the great city itself. San Francisco is one of the largest and most exciting cities in the United States, yet preserves its old world charm in a spectacular natural setting.

Leaving the city by the iconic Golden Gate Bridge, the route meanders northwards through affluent Marin County, along a lengthy stretch of exceptional coastline to the Point Reyes National Seashore. Here, the wind- and wave-whipped rocks are home to a colony of elephant seals. At Point Arena, an elegant lighthouse can be climbed to an observation deck for incredible views.

This swathe of northern California is sometimes known as the 'Redwood Empire', for its forests of *Sequoiadendron giganteum*, one of the tallest and largest species of tree in the world that reaches heights of 75–100 metres (250–330ft). The famous 'Avenue of the Giants' begins just north of tiny Philipsville, a 50-kilometre (30-mile) section of the old Highway 101 lined with mammoth trees. The Avenue is surrounded by the vast Humboldt Redwoods State Park, which has the largest remaining stand of virgin redwoods in the world. Many of these trees have stood here for more than a thousand years.

The Pacific Ocean turns golden in a sunset viewed from McWay Falls in Julia Pfeiffer Burns State Park. This park, near Big Sur, is one of many state parks lining the Pacific Coast Highway.

TRAVELLER'S TIPS

Best time to go: The best time to travel is in spring and autumn. Summers are hot and the roads are busy, while winters are mild but rainy.

Look out for: Road damage after severe weather conditions. Some stretches have been prone to flooding and rockslides.

Dos and don'ts: Do respect the wildlife. Bears and elephant seals are among the wildlife along this route that can behave aggressively if disturbed.

THE ROCKIES BY TRAIN

Start Calgary   **End** Vancouver   **Countries crossed** Canada

Distance 1,088 kilometres (676 miles)   **Transport used** Train

Highlights Incredible mountain scenery, wildlife, Lake Louise train station, Spiral Tunnels, Stoney Creek Bridge, Craigellachie 'Last Spike', Thompson River Canyon, Vancouver

In 1885, the Canadian Pacific Railway completed the country's first transcontinental railway line, crossing vast plains, mountains, rivers and lakes to link the Atlantic and Pacific coasts. It was the longest railway ever constructed at the time of its completion, and the remarkable feat involved 12,000 men, 5,000 horses, 300 dog-sled teams, more than four years and almost $50,000,000. Although it has been closed to ordinary passenger traffic since 1990, it is now possible to take luxurious touring trains along the historic line. There are several routes available, but this journey follows the classic Kicking Horse route, named for a vertiginous mountain pass high in the Rocky Mountains. The trip takes two days. The Rocky Mountaineer trains include observation cars with wraparound windows, offering incomparable views of the scenery. Travellers will see some of the large mammals for which the Rockies are famous, including bears, elk, deer, moose, mountain goats and bighorn sheep.

The journey begins in Calgary, a sleepy agricultural town before the arrival of the railway in 1883, but now the largest city in the Canadian province of Alberta. The famous Calgary Stampede, a rodeo exhibition and festival that takes place every July, developed from a local agricultural fair first held in the 1880s. The train soon leaves the grasslands of the Prairies behind, and makes the climb into the Rockies. The first stop is at Banff, the highest town in Canada and the gateway to the spectacular Banff National Park. The journey continues along Bow River, lined with dense forest and set against a backdrop of dramatic peaks. At Lake Louise, it passes the beautifully restored wooden station built by the Canadian Pacific Railway, which was used as a set in David Lean's 1965 film *Doctor Zhivago*. A few minutes later the train passes the Continental Divide: east of this natural boundary, water flows towards the Atlantic; to the west, it flows into the Pacific. At 1,625 metres (5,330 ft), this is the highest point of the journey.

The turquoise Moraine Lake nestles in the Valley of the Ten Peaks in Banff National Park. Many travellers arrange to break the train journey here to explore the stunning scenery by car.

TRAVELLER'S TIPS

Best time to go: June is the most beautiful month to cross the Rockies, with spring in full swing, but with snow still capping the mountains. July and August are the busiest months.

Look out for: Rocky Mountaineer trains only run between April and October.

Dos and don'ts: Do remember to turn your watches back one hour at the border with Alberta.

The Spiral Tunnels were built in 1907 to replace a dangerously steep stretch of track. The train enters the first tunnel and makes a complete loop to emerge facing in the opposite direction, before entering the second tunnel and performing the same manoeuvre. The train continues past the Kicking Horse River, one of the most beautiful stretches of this panoramic route.

Around lunchtime, the train reaches Stoney Creek Bridge, a handsome 200-metre (600-ft)-high arched steel bridge built in 1929, which replaced an earlier wooden construction. This is a celebrated picture spot, and the sight of the train curving into the approach to the bridge is perhaps the most famous image of the journey.

Downtown Vancouver, with False Creek in the foreground, a narrow inlet that separates the downtown area from the rest of the city. This busy city at the foot of the Rockies is a major port and logging centre, but combines heavy industry with one of the highest standards of city living in the world.

In mid afternoon the train passes Craigellachie, where the last spike of the Canadian Pacific Railway was hammered into place on 7 November 1885, finally linking Canada's Atlantic and Pacific coasts. It follows the shores of Lake Shuswap, where the huge, untidy nests of osprey can be spotted among the trees, on to Lake Mara, where the scenery becomes softer and less dramatic. The day culminates at Kamloops, a large city at the confluence of the North and South Thompson rivers.

On the second day, the train follows the river to reach the shores of Kamloops Lake, where bald eagles soar over steep, rugged embankments. It passes through the Black Canyon, named for the undulating black lava cliffs, and the dramatic Thompson River Canyon. At Avalanche Alley, the tracks are bounded on one side by sheer rock, and run thrillingly close to the river on the other. The Thompson flows into the Fraser

River, which rushes through the narrow pass at Hell's Gate, where a suspension footbridge spans the river.

The last stretch heads through increasingly flat farmland before making the approach to Vancouver. The train terminates at a beautifully converted 1950s locomotive maintenance building in the heart of the city. Although the journey may be over, take time to explore the magnificent city of Vancouver, which combines all the attractions of a metropolis – great museums and galleries, fine dining and excellent nightlife – with a scenic location on the beautiful Burrard Peninsula on Canada's Pacific coast. The distant Rockies provide a theatrical backdrop to the glossy skyscrapers concentrated in the downtown area, and, if the big city attractions should ever pall, there are extensive parks and pristine coastline within easy reach.

Northern Lights glow spectacularly in the skies over Banff National Park. These are most likely to be seen around the time of the equinox in late September.

THE APPALACHIAN TRAIL

Mt Katahdin

Pine Grove
Furnace
State Park

Springer Mountain

Start Springer Mountain, Georgia
End Mount Katahdin, Maine

Countries crossed USA

Distance 3,510 kilometres (2,180 miles)

Transport used By foot

Highlights Wildlife, Chattahoochee National
Forest, Great Smoky Mountains National
Park, McAfee Knob, Delaware Water Gap,
White Mountain National Forest,
100-Mile Wilderness

The Appalachian Trail, North America's most famous long-distance hiking path, follows the ridge of the Appalachian Mountains. Remarkably, although it stretches all the way from Georgia to Maine, the trail keeps largely to unspoilt wilderness. Almost all of the trail is protected in nature reserves. Most of the 4 million people who visit the trail annually walk just a small section, but the fabled 'thru-hikers' hike its entire length in a single season, starting in Georgia in early spring and finishing in Maine when the leaves turn crimson and gold. It's no mean feat: the elevation gain and loss over the entire trail is said to equal ascending and descending Mount Everest 16 times.

The southern trailhead is Springer Mountain, part of Georgia's Blue Range Mountains, so-called for their bluish hue when viewed from a distance. From there, the trail meanders through the magnificent Chattahoochee National Forest. Some of the finest scenery of the southern Appalachians can be experienced on the often demanding route through Tennessee's Great Smoky Mountains National Park, and in North Carolina's Pisgah National Forest.

About a quarter of the trail is found in Virginia, where forested mountain peaks and crags such as McAfee Knob offer unforgettable vistas, and rhododendrons and azaleas blaze into bloom in summer. The trail crosses the Potomac River into West Virginia and on to Maryland, where the route threads along the ridge crest of South Mountain. In Pennsylvania, the Pine Grove Furnace State Park marks the halfway point. The trail continues north into the busier and more accessible sections of the route that traverse the states of New York and New Jersey. The wooded valleys of Massachusetts are overlooked by two of the most dramatic peaks on the trail, Mt Greylock and Mt Everett. The remote slopes of Vermont's Green Mountains live up to their name, with tangled woods and verdant pastures. Some of the most demanding sections are found in New Hampshire's White Mountain National Forest, where much of the trail unfolds above the treeline. Maine boasts the Appalachian's most isolated stretch in the so-called '100-Mile Wilderness', and its highest mountain, Mt Katahdin, which is the stunning culmination to the trail.

Here, the trees are in full autumn splendour in New Hampshire's White Mountains National Forest. The trail climbs well above the treeline through this section, which is more than 160 kilometres (100 miles) long.

TRAVELLER'S **TIPS**

Best time to go: The trail can be hiked at any time from spring to autumn; the season is slightly shorter in the north of the trail, where higher altitudes mean longer winters.

Look out for: Several species of venomous snakes, including rattlesnakes and copperheads, are found along the trail. Poison ivy is a common nuisance.

Dos and don'ts: Do be aware that permits are required to hike certain sections of the trail, including the Great Smoky Mountains National Park (North Carolina and Tennessee) and Shenandoah National Park (Virginia). Do ensure that you are carrying enough drinking water.

THE YUCATÁN PENINSULA

Start Mérida, Mexico
End Tikal, Guatemala

Countries crossed Mexico, Guatemala,

Distance 1,440 kilometres (895 miles)

Transport used Local buses

Highlights Mérida, Chichén Itzá, Uxmal,
Campeche, San Cristóbal de las Casas,
Palenque, Flores, Tikal, Copán

The Mayan civilization, which flourished between the third and tenth centuries, was one of the most advanced of Mesoamerica. The remains of the Mayans' cities display extraordinary technical, mathematical and astronomical prowess. This journey explores some of the greatest Mayan cities ever built, travelling down the Yucatán peninsula into Guatemala.

The Mexican capital of Yucatán is Mérida, founded by Spanish explorers in 1542 on the site of the ancient Mayan city of T'ho. Even now, carved Mayan stones are found incorporated into some of the city's oldest buildings, including the cathedral. The city boasts a well preserved historic quarter, replete with colonial churches and palaces, and makes a fine base for visiting the nearby Mayan temples of Chichén Itzá and Uxmal.

Chichén Itzá is one of the most spectacular complexes of the Mayan civilization, a city of stone dominating an arid plain. The centrepiece of the complex is the Temple of Kukulkan, a huge stepped temple which, at 24 metres (79 ft), is the tallest building on the site. It was dedicated to the Mayan snake deity Kukulkan. The monumental staircase on the northern flank is adorned by a carved balustrade that culminates in a snake head with gaping jaws. On the equinoxes, a shadow strikes the staircase creating the illusion of a snake slithering down the side of the temple.

Set amid jungle-clad hills in northern Guatemala, the ruins of Tikal contain some of the largest pre-Columbian buildings in the Americas. The central temple complex has been thoroughly excavated, but an estimated 50 sq kilometres (20 sq mi) of the city remains hidden by the vegetation.

Best time to go: The best time of year is between November and March, which is neither too hot nor too wet.

Look out for: Note that rental cars cannot be taken across international borders in this region. The sites described are all reached by public bus and local tours.

Dos and don'ts: Do check up-to-date travel information. Weather damage and political turmoil can affect travel in this region.

Many streets of fine Spanish colonial architecture survive in Mérida, the capital of Yucatán province. Founded in 1542, Mérida is the oldest continually occupied city in the Americas.

Uxmal is located in the Puuc hills south of Mérida, and was largely constructed at the end of the ninth century, when it was the capital of a thriving city-state. The buildings are the finest examples of Puuc construction techniques, developed to accommodate the contours of the hills, and characterized by precisely cut veneer stones pressed into a concrete core. Continue to Campeche, an elegant preserved colonial town overlooking the Gulf of Mexico. Founded in 1540 by the Spanish conquistadors, it was built over the ruins of the Mayan city of Canpech, of which almost nothing has survived. The journey south from Campeche is long, so travellers often stay overnight in the big, modern city of Villahermosa, before pressing on to charming colonial town of San Cristóbal de las Casas, set in a verdant valley in the Chiapas highlands.

Deep in the Chiapas jungle, Palenque emerges like a mirage from the vegetation that has claimed most of the city. Only a small section has been excavated, but the buildings exhibit some of the finest architecture of the Mayan civilization. Palenque flourished in the seventh century, when it was an important ceremonial centre and provincial capital. Its finest building is the extraordinary Temple of the Inscriptions, built as a funerary monument for the city's legendary ruler, Pacal the Great. Its inner walls are covered with inscriptions, which have proved the key to deciphering ancient Mayan.

Head east into Guatemala and the little town of Flores, which occupies an island on Lake Petén. Flores is the main base for visiting Tikal and other Mayan sites near the border with Belize. Tikal was capital of one of the largest city-states of the Mayan empire, which reached its apogee between the third and tenth centuries. The pyramid-shaped temples are the most impressive surviving structures, including one (Temple IV) that, at 70 metres (230 ft) high, is the tallest pre-Columbian structure in the Americas. Tikal is the centrepiece of a national park, which also protects the smaller ruins of Uaxactún. More extraordinary ruins lie farther east in the Cultural Triangle Yaxhá Nakum-Naranjo National Park.

The temple complex of Chichén Itzá sits in an arid plain in northern Yucatán. This reclining figure is known as a Chac-Mool, a type of Mayan statue that probably had religious significance, although its original purpose is unknown.

PARC NATIONAL DU BIC TO CARLETON

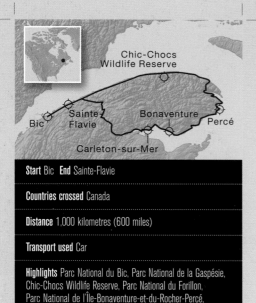

Chic-Chocs
Wildlife Reserve

Bonaventure

Bic

Sainte-
Flavie

Percé

Carleton-sur-Mer

Start Bic   End Sainte-Flavie
Countries crossed Canada
Distance 1,000 kilometres (600 miles)
Transport used Car
Highlights Parc National du Bic, Parc National de la Gaspésie, Chic-Chocs Wildlife Reserve, Parc National du Forillon, Parc National de l'Île-Bonaventure-et-du-Rocher-Percé, Carleton-sur-Mer, Matapédia valley

Quebec's Gaspé Peninsula marks one end of the beautiful Appalachian Mountains. This enchanting region is sparsely populated, but its rugged coastline and forested mountain interior are home to abundant wildlife, including black bear, red fox, moose, lynx, beaver, deer and caribou. A glorious coastal road, Route 132, circumnavigates the peninsula, passing coves, fishing villages, nature reserves and beaches, providing scope for fishing, bird-watching, hiking, swimming, kayaking and many other activities.

The village of Bic, on the southern bank of the St Lawrence Estuary, is the gateway to the magnificent Parc National du Bic. Forested slopes tumble into rocky bays. Hiking trails lead to clifftop lookouts, where you can watch the sun dip below the horizon. From Bic, head east following the St Lawrence River towards Sainte-Flavie, the first town in the Gaspé Peninsula proper. Just beyond Mont Joli, stop to admire the Redford Gardens, first laid out in the 1920s. The cliffs pitch ever more steeply as the road continues eastwards, twisting and turning. The Parc National de la Gaspésie, accessed inland from Sainte Anne des Monts, offers breathtaking vistas, while the adjacent Chic-Chocs Wildlife Reserve shelters moose, black bear, snowshoe hare and porcupine.

The eastern point of the peninsula is the most dramatic, with thrusting mountains and jagged capes. The Parc National du Forillon occupies a narrow, wooded headland, where seabirds nest in towering cliffs, and beavers toil at their dams on rivers and streams. Next to isolated Percé village, the famous Percé Rock juts up from the bay, and is protected by the spectacular Parc National de l'Île-Bonaventure-et-du-Rocher-Percé. Long beaches stretch along the Baie des Chaleurs on the peninsula's southern coast, where charming villages are linked by coastal walking and biking paths. Next to Carleton-sur-Mer, a fishing village-cum-beach resort, you'll find the Parc National de Miguasha, which has been recognized by UNESCO for its wealth of fossils, which shed remarkable light on the history of the Earth.

Route 132 winds through the idyllic Matapédia Valley, famous for its excellent salmon fishing, before returning to Sainte-Flavie on the northern coast.

The Percé Rock in the foreground rises vertiginously 438 metres (1,437 ft) from the sea on the remote eastern end of the peninsula. Beyond the Percé Rock stand the Three Sisters cliffs.

TRAVELLER'S **TIPS**

Best time to go: The best time to visit is between May to October. Hikers will enjoy the autumn colours in September and October. Spring, and to a lesser extent autumn, are best for spotting migratory birds, while whale-watching is best between June and July.

Look out for: Interpretation centres on reserve lands in the Gaspé Peninsula provide opportunities for learning more about the ancient culture of the Mi'kmaq communities.

Dos and don'ts: Do bring picnic lunches as it is hard to find restaurants outside the main towns. Don't disturb local wildlife, particularly nesting seabirds.

COSTA RICA

Start San José **End** San José	
Countries crossed Costa Rica	
Distance 860 kilometers (530 miles)	
Transport used 4×4, boat	
Highlights San José, Arenal Volcano, Monteverde Cloud Forest Preserve, Manuel Antonio National Park, whitewater rafting, turtle nesting grounds on the Tortuguero National Park	

Costa Rica is one of the most ecologically diverse regions on Earth, with habitats of pristine cloud forest and Caribbean beaches. Approximately a quarter of the country is protected in conservation areas. Starting in San José, this journey makes a figure-of-eight loop around some of the country's most extraordinary sights.

The sprawling capital San José sits at the nexus of most major roads in the middle of the expansive Central Plain. The city was founded by the Spanish in the late 18th century, and preserves a smattering of historic buildings. There are a clutch of excellent museums, including the Museum of Precolumbian Gold, which displays more than 2,000 dazzling treasures.

San José is ringed by volcanic mountains. The Arenal National Park, named after the country's most active volcano, is located a 3–4 hour drive north of the city. Arenal erupted in 1968 after lying dormant for four centuries, and is currently one of the most active volcanoes in the world, emitting spurts of smoke and lava almost daily. Several natural hot springs dot the park, ranging from simple pools to lavish spa complexes. There is no accommodation within the park, but the nearby town of Fortuna contains hotels and restaurants.

The drive from Fortuna to the next destination, the cloud forest of Monteverde, borders Lake Arenal, the largest lake in the country. The road loops around the lake to reach Tilarán. From here, a 4×4 is recommended for the steep drive into the mountains.

Cost Rica's conservation areas support more than 500,000 species of flora and fauna in their dense rainforest, including the red-eyed tree frog, pictured here at La Selva Biological Research Station.

Best time to go: The dry season (December to April) is the most popular time to visit the country, but coming in the rainy season has several advantages, not least the possibility of seeing turtles in their Caribbean nesting grounds.

Look out for: This route can be driven in a 4×4 or you could take advantage of the country's shuttle bus system or private taxis.

Dos and don'ts: Do reserve admission to the parks in advance, particularly at Monteverde which only allows 100 people on the trails at a time.

Arenal Volcano, 90 kilometres (55 miles) northwest of San José, is a volcano 1,633 metres (5,358 ft) high. After centuries of inactivity, the volcano erupted in 1968, destroying the nearby town of Tabacón, and it has been constantly active ever since. Arenal is also known as the 'Sugar Loaf' due to its conical shape.

Cloud forests, found on the slopes of mountains in tropical regions, are the most luxuriant of tropical forests. Perpetually swathed in cloud, they draw in moisture to create a habitat where mosses, lichens and ferns thrive. The Monteverde Cloud Forest Preserve extends over 10,500 hectares (26,000 acres), with elfin woodlands on the highest peaks, and vine-draped rainforest at lower elevations. Rivers and waterfalls abound, and the humid conditions are ideally suited to bromeliads and orchids. Among the wildlife found here are jaguars, ocelots, tapirs and more than 400 species of bird, including the elusive quetzal, famous for its brightly coloured plumage.

From Monteverde, continue south to the town of Quepos, gateway to Manuel Antonio National Park. This is Costa Rica's smallest national preserve, but also one of the most visited, its idyllic Pacific coastline backed by extensive tropical forest. Costa Rica's road system means that you will have to return to San José before heading west on the next loop of this journey. From San José, drive east to Turrialbo, which is a big hub for whitewater rafting tours. Just north of Turrialbo is the Guayabo National Monument, a partially excavated city built by a long-gone civilization more than 3,000 years ago.

Continue to Moín, just north of Limón on the Caribbean coast. This is the starting point for boats to the Tortuguero National Park, one of the most isolated and beautiful areas in the country. Tortuguero means 'turtle-catcher', and the park provides one of the most important nesting sites of the endangered green sea turtle, which lays its eggs here between July and October. Three other turtle species also nest here. The remote marshes and lagoons shelter a remarkable variety of other wildlife, including endangered mammals such as the jaguar, sloth, tapir and manatee. After exploring this remote wilderness, return to the busy capital where the journey ends.

The Manuel Antonio National Park, on Costa Rica's Pacific coastline, boasts beautiful beaches backing onto dense tropical forests. There are numerous hiking trails through the park, which can be tackled independently or with the assistance of a guide.

THE CARIBBEAN ISLANDS

Start Havana **End** Tobago	

Countries crossed Cuba, Jamaica, Dominican Republic, Puerto Rico, Virgin Islands, French Caribbean, Trinidad and Tobago

Distance 2,140 kilometres (1,300 miles) **Transport used** Yacht, ferry, plane

Highlights Beaches, watersports, carnivals and festivals, nature reserves

The long chain of Caribbean islands stretch for more than 4,000 kilometres (2,500 miles) around the Caribbean Sea. There are more than 7,000 islands, ranging from uninhabited islets to sizeable island nations. A dizzying range of languages, customs and cuisines awaits the traveller on land, while the turquoise seas and colourful reefs reveal a dazzling sub-aquatic world. This journey hops between some of the largest islands in the chain, and can be made by local plane (the most common option), by ferry or, ideally, by yacht.

Begin the journey in Cuba, renowned for its rich musical heritage and the faded glamour of its capital city, Havana, whose old quarter, Old Havana, is a crumbling maze of Spanish colonial mansions and faded churches, where battered Russian cars and vintage Cadillacs clatter through the streets. From Cuba, hop across to Jamaica. The indigenous islanders named it Xaymaca, meaning the 'Land of Forests and Springs', and shadowy peaks stretch along its spine. You can hike up through coffee plantations to the summit of the Blue Mountain for incredible views over the island. The coastline is blessed with extraordinary beaches, including the famously

The Plaza de la Catedral ['Cathedral Square'] is one of five squares in Old Havana. Many of the area's fine old buildings have fallen into a dangerous state of disrepair, but a programme of regeneration is restoring them.

TRAVELLER'S **TIPS**

Best time to go: The winter months are ideal, but avoid hurricane season (June to November) if possible.

Look out for: Ensure you have all relevant visas, as you will be hopping between several countries and passing through numerous border controls.

Dos and don'ts: Do find out about local festivals before arrival.

Saona Island is an idyllic tropical island just off the southeastern tip of the Dominican Republic. It is a protected nature reserve and is famous for the natural beauty of its beaches, where sea life flourishes in the warm, shallow waters.

hedonistic Seven Mile Beach in the northwest of the island at Negril, while Frenchman's Cove and the Blue Lagoon are perfect for stringing up a hammock and drowsing away an afternoon.

Next, head east to another former Spanish colony, the Dominican Republic. The capital, Santo Domingo, is a quirky fusion of worn Spanish architecture and relaxed island traditions. There are fabulous beaches at the easternmost tip of the country at Punta Cana. It's a quick skip across to Puerto Rico, where the idyllic islands of Vieques and Culebra entice visitors with their immaculate beaches, while the Cordillera mountains and rainforest provide a tranquil retreat.

Continue east to the Virgin Islands. This archipelago of mountainous isles is shared by the USA and the UK, and is one of the world's foremost sailing destinations. Much of the island of St John is a protected nature park. In Trunk Bay, snorkellers can follow an underwater trail that reveals a wonderland of tropical fish. Some of the best beaches are found on Tortola, in the British Virgin Islands, where Cane Garden Bay is regularly voted one of the finest in the world.

Next along the chain, the islands of the French Caribbean, including Guadeloupe, Martinique and St Barts, are among the choicest holiday destinations in the region. Just east, Antigua's sparkling white sands and pristine reefs are spectacularly beautiful. Nearby Barbados combines a dramatic mountainous hinterland with elegant towns, replete with colonial architecture.

The most northerly of the Windward Islands, Santa Lucia is refreshingly unspoilt, with towering mountains, lush

rainforest and stunning beaches. Every year from March to May, giant leatherback turtles lumber on to the Grand Anse beach to lay their eggs. South of Santa Lucia, St Vincent is theatrically crowned by a smoking volcano, La Soufrière, which can be hiked for a giddy glimpse into the caldera. Grenada, at the southernmost tip of the Windward Island archipelago, is known as the 'Spice Island' for its extensive plantations of cloves, nutmeg, cinnamon and ginger. A large swathe of the island is protected in the Grand Etang National Park, a breathtaking natural wilderness encompassing rivers, lakes, waterfalls, rainforest and rugged peaks. There are more stunning beaches, including the superb Grand Anse, an endless stretch of dazzling white sand.

Trinidad and Tobago lie just off the coast of Venezuela, and are the most ethnically diverse of the Caribbean islands. Lively Trinidad is famous for its explosive carnival celebrations, while sleepy Tobago is a tropical dream, with white sand beaches and superb reefs where manta rays flap among the multi-hued fish. This is the perfect end to a Caribbean odyssey.

The annual Trinidad and Tobago carnival takes place over two days before the start of Lent. The highlight of the islands' calendar, with elaborate costumes, calypso bands, stickfighting and limbo dancing, the Trinidad carnival is one of the oldest, biggest and most spectacular carnivals in the world.

THE AMAZON

Anavilhanas Archipelago

Manaus

Novo Airão

Encontro das Águas

Start Manaus **End** Manaus	
Countries crossed Brazil	
Distance 250 kilometres (150 miles)	
Transport used Boat	
Highlights Amazonian wildlife, Anavilhanas Archipelago, Encontro das Águas	

The mighty River Amazon is the second-longest on Earth, spanning the borders of eight countries including Brazil, Peru, Bolivia, Ecuador and Colombia. From its source high in the Peruvian Andes, it travels for 6,800 kilometres (4,200 miles)

Sky and clouds reflected in the slow-moving current of the River Amazon. Despite being one of the world's longest rivers, at no point is it spanned by any bridge, both because of its width and because it passes through dense, unpopulated rainforest with few roads.

through the world's largest tropical rainforest before disgorging into the Atlantic Ocean. The Amazon Basin (which encompasses the area covered by the river and its tributaries) covers almost 40 per cent of South America and sustains a staggeringly rich diversity of flora and fauna. This week-long river journey begins and ends in Manaus, which is the main hub for Amazon river cruises, but extends into little-visited regions replete with astonishing plant, bird and animal life. It also affords opportunities to see the three different types of forest typical of the Amazon basin: the seasonally flooded Igapó and Varzea forests, and the tall Terre Firme forest.

Manaus, capital of the state of Amazonas, is a large, dynamic city located at the confluence of the Negro and Solimoes rivers, two of the Amazon's biggest tributaries. Established in 1699 by Portuguese slave-traders, the city flourished during the 19th-century rubber boom, when it was endowed with extravagant villas and a magnificent opera house. When the rubber industry collapsed (after rubber plant seeds were smuggled out of the country, ending Brazil's monopoly)

the city fell into decline, and modern Manaus is sprawling and chaotic. The main sights are clustered in the historic centre, and include the elegant 19th-century Customs House and Justice Palace, and the delicate glass-and-wrought-iron municipal market, which is a copy of Les Halles in Paris. The enormous port is the main transport hub for the upper Amazon Basin, and filled with huge cruise ships, traditional double-decker riverboats, and the dug-out canoes used by local people who come to trade goods and pick up supplies. The city has preserved vast swathes of native forest in protected parks and even here, on the very fringes of the bustling city, it is possible to glimpse several species of wildlife.

The first day on board the riverboat is spent travelling up the Rio Negro, one of the biggest Amazonian tributaries, cruising through the Anavilhanas, the world's largest freshwater archipelago, made up of more than 400 islands. Dragonflies with shimmering wings dart across the river, where huge *Victoria amazonica* water lilies unfurl their enormous leaves. In the evening, the fortunate might glimpse the endangered

The Anavilhanas Archipelago is a huge expanse of flooded rainforest in the Rio Negro, covering an area of 350,000 hectares (850,000 acres). During the rainy season, more than half of the islands are submerged. Here, the waters seem dark because of humic acid from decomposing vegetation.

pink river dolphin, or one of several species of monkey and sloth that inhabit the dense canopies of the pristine forest. These islands are a paradise for bird-watchers, and parrots, macaws, toucans and herons are commonly sighted.

The following day might begin with an early morning canoe trip close to the forest edge. The diversity of plant species in the Amazonian rainforest is the highest on Earth, and a single kilometre contains more than a thousand types of trees and thousands of species of other higher plants, all thriving in the intense humidity. After lunch, consider a cooling dip in the river: the infamous piranha, despite its fearsome reputation, is more partial to fruit than to human flesh and the tea-coloured waters are some of the cleanest to be found anywhere. More forest exploration is followed by dinner on board the river boat, as the distant guttural cry of the howler monkey is joined by the shriek of macaws, and frogs add an insistent, throbbing chorus.

The third and fourth days are spent travelling farther upriver, with stops for wildlife-spotting either in a small boat along the water's edge, or on foot into the forest. There are more than 350 indigenous ethnic groups living in the Amazon, of which it is estimated that at least 100 groups remain uncontacted. Along this stretch of the Rio Negro, the boat passes a smattering of small villages, clusters of simple wooden structures topped with grass roofs, surrounded by small fields for vegetable cultivation. Dug-out canoes – used for fishing, hunting and trading goods with other communities – are tethered to the shore. Visits to indigenous villages can be arranged, and the locals will describe their customs and legends, their crops and the medicinal uses of the plants they gather. At the confluence of the Rio Negro and the Rio Jaueperi, the Iguapó flooded forest provides incomparable opportunities for wildlife-spotting, particularly at night, when the guides hunt for the glimmering eyes of caiman and other creatures using searchlights.

The return voyage down the Rio Negro follows the western bank, and stops at Novo Airão, about 100 kilometres (60 miles) northwest of Manaus. Founded by the Jesuits in the late 17th century, you can explore the remains of Velha Airão (the original settlement) and watch dolphins cavorting in the harbour. Before docking at Manaus, the boat descends to the famous Encontro das Águas ('Meeting of the Waters'), where the dark brown waters of the Rio Negro meet the creamy, silt-laden waters of the Solimões, the two continuing in parallel for several kilometres.

The Amazon rainforest contains the most diverse range of flora and fauna in the world. There are more than 1,300 species of bird, including the noisy, colourful scarlet macaw.

46

EL CHEPE

Start Chihuahua **End** Los Mochis	
Countries crossed Mexico	
Distance 670 kilometres (415 miles)	
Transport used Train	
Highlights Cascada de Basaseachi, Arareco Lake, Cusarare and Basaseachi waterfalls, Urique Canyon, cave homes of the Tarahumara people, hiking and horse-riding trails	

The Sierra Madre mountain range in northwestern Mexico is deeply scored with a network of gorges, collectively known as the Barranca del Cobre ('Copper Canyon'). The best way to explore the region is to take the 'El Chepe' Railroad from Chihuahua to Los Mochis near the Gulf of California.

The state capital of Chihuahua is the starting point of the journey, a sprawling modern city smattered with examples of Spanish colonial architecture. From there, the train ascends through arid desert to the foothills of the Sierra Madre. The plains give way to rugged hills wrapped in pine forest as the train climbs to Creel, gateway to the Sierra Tarahumara (the name for this western swathe of the Sierra Madre).

The train pauses briefly at Divisadero, allowing visitors to gaze over the lip of the magnificent Urique Canyon, the central gorge of the system, which plunges dramatically for almost 1,900 metres (6,200 ft). Travellers who stay overnight can follow local hiking trails to the Piedra Volada waterfall and the cave dwellings of the Tarahumara people. At Bauichivo, the next station stop, visitors can alight for the former missionary settlement of Cerocahui and hike or ride deep into the canyons.

The most scenic section of the journey is next, as the train winds through narrow gorges rimmed with craggy rocks, lumbers through tunnels, and crosses sparkling emerald lakes. In late summer, the meadows are carpeted with flowers. The drama diminishes as the train emerges from the Sierra Madre to reach El Fuerte, another fine old colonial settlement. The terminus is Los Mochis, a dusty agricultural town. There, bus connections link to the seaside at Topolobambo, where dolphins skim across the bay.

The Basaseachic Falls, at 246 metres (807 ft) the highest waterfall in Mexico to flow all year round, is easily accessible from a base in the nearby town of Creel.

TRAVELLER'S **TIPS**

Best time to go: The best time to visit is late spring and early summer, when the meadows are full of flowers and the rivers and waterfalls are still full.

Look out for: It is possible to make the entire journey in a single day, but ideally travellers should stop along the way to visit the local villages and explore the canyons.

Dos and don'ts: Do purchase first class tickets in advance; second class tickets can be bought on the train. Do consider booking a guide when hiking, as trails are poorly marked.

THE INCA TRAIL

Machu Picchu

Km 82

Start Km 82 **End** Machu Picchu

Countries crossed Peru

Distance 43 kilometres (26 miles)

Transport used On foot

Highlights Llaqtapata, Warmiwañusca (also known as Dead Woman's Pass), Runkuracay, Phuyupatamarca and Wiñaywayna, Machu Picchu

The royal city of Machu Picchu, high in the remote peaks of the Peruvian Andes, is one of the greatest achievements of the Inca civilization. Built in the 1400s, but abandoned after the arrival of the Spanish conquistadors a century later, it was lost to the outside world for more than 500 years. Now the breathtaking ruins of this mysterious city, arranged along a steep ridge over the Urubamba Valley, provide the climax of the celebrated Inca Trail, a demanding hike along ancient mountain routes. Although there are variations on the trail, the Classic Route is the most popular, combining dramatic mountain scenery and cloud forest with haunting Inca ruins. The route covers 43 kilometres (26 miles) at altitudes of up to 4,200 metres (13,800 ft), and usually takes four days.

Cuzco, at 3,400 metres (11,200 ft) above sea level, was the historic capital of the Inca Empire. Now the main base for visiting Machu Picchu, travellers are advised to spend a few days here in order to acclimatize before tackling the Inca Trail. But practicality isn't the only reason to spend time in Cuzco: this beautiful city, replete with ancient ruins and Spanish colonial architecture, provides an ideal introduction into the enigmatic world of the Incas. Their empire once encompassed a 3,000-km (2,000-mile)-long swathe of western South America and their language – Quechua – remains the most widely spoken indigenous language in the Americas. The walled fortress of Sacsayhuamán on the outskirts of Cuzco displays their sophisticated engineering skills, with each huge stone neatly slotted into the next without the aid of mortar.

The most common trailhead for the Classic Route is at Kilometre 82, so-named for its distance along the rail line from Cuzco. The first day's trek is comparatively gentle, descending into the Urumbaya canyon, still etched with Inca terraces. A small detour along the rushing Cusichaca River will bring you to the neat ruins of Llaqtapata ('Terrace Town'), a riverside farming settlement. Camp is struck that night at Huayllabamba, the last inhabited village along the route.

TRAVELLER'S TIPS

Best time to go: May is an ideal month to hike the trail, with fewer crowds and spring vegetation; July and August are the busiest months. The trail is closed in February.

Look out for: Be sure to acclimatize in Cuzco; altitude sickness is rare but can affect some unprepared hikers.

Dos and don'ts: Do book 2–3 months in advance to do the trek, as only 500 people a day, including guides and porters, are allowed.

Hundreds of different species of orchid grow in the region around Machu Picchu, many of them on the site itself, where you will also find bromeliads and other flowering plants. Flower-lovers can also take in the Orchid Trail, a collection of native orchids in the grounds of the Inkaterra Machu Picchu Pueblo Hotel in Cuzco.

Much of the route along the Inca Trail follows the original Inca roads. The Inca did not use wheeled transport, so the roads were designed for people on foot and pack animals.

The second day is the toughest, with a gruelling ascent up to Warmiwañusca, also known as Dead Woman's Pass, which is the highest pass on the route. The views of the surrounding peaks are mesmerizing. From here the route begins to dip, and the arid slopes give way to verdant forest. The night is spent in the Pacamayo Valley.

On the third day, the route continues up the valley, climbing towards another panoramic pass. The climb is less arduous, and the journey is broken about half way up by a visit to Runkuracay, which functioned as a small Inca lookout point and staging post for couriers. This circular vantage point offers a stunning view back to Warmiwañusca and over the Pacamayo Valley below. Beyond the pass, the route picks up the Inca road, made centuries ago from huge blocks of hand-hewn stone. Astonishingly, the Incas built about 23,000 kilometres (14,000 miles) of these stone trails, which crisscrossed the length and breadth of their enormous empire. Several more ruins await, including Sayaqmarca ('Inaccessible Town'). Surrounded on three sides by sheer cliffs, it is arranged in terraces on a narrow spur jutting out over the Aobamba Valley. At the top of the third pass, romantically overgrown Phuyupatamarca ('Town Above the Clouds') peeks out from wisps of mist and is ringed with lofty peaks. The path, which now resembles a sturdy stone staircase, descends through lush cloud forest to the extensive remains of Wiñaywayna ('Forever Young'), a stone labyrinth of homes, bathhouses and temples.

Most hikers make a pre-dawn start on the fourth day, hoping to reach Machu Picchu at sunrise. The Sun Gate, at the top of a ridge, affords the first views of the spellbinding stone citadel. Although the origins of this vast estate are still shrouded in uncertainty, it is widely believed that Machu Picchu was built as a winter palace for the great Inca emperor Pachacuti (1438–72). Many believe that the city also functioned as an important pilgrimage centre dedicated to Inca divinities. There are more than 200 structures within the complex, but the finest – and most enigmatic – are clustered in the Sacred District. The Temple of the Sun and the Room of the Three Windows are dedicated to the sun god Inti, from whom the Inca leaders were said to have descended. The Intihuatana, a carved sacred stone which functions as an astronomical 'clock', is the only such Inca stone to have survived the Spanish conquistadors, and retains enormous religious significance for locals. The journey ends with the train ride back to Cuzco.

TO THE ENDS OF THE WORLD

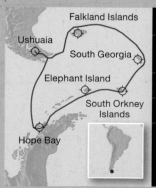

Start Ushuaia **End** Ushuaia	
Countries crossed Argentina, United Kingdom, Antarctica	
Distance 6,330 kilometres (3,930 miles)	
Transport used Ship	
Highlights Ushuaia, Falkland Islands, Antarctic Convergence, South Georgia, South Orkney Islands, Elephant Island, South Shetland Islands, Hope Bay on the Antarctic mainland	

This voyage to the great white continent of Antarctica follows in the footsteps of some of the world's greatest explorers. Most of this distant polar region has never been inhabited by humans, yet these majestic lands are home to an incredible variety of bird and animal life.

Ushuaia is the capital of Argentina's Tierra del Fuego province, and the most southerly city in the world. It sits curled around a wide bay, backed by snow-capped mountains. The city is a popular hub for ecotourism, with excursions to the surrounding fjords and glaciers as well as to

TRAVELLER'S **TIPS**

Best time to go: Antarctica is accessible only from November to March as the seas are impassable in winter.

Look out for: Even the hardiest sailors will feel nauseous during severe storms, so ensure that you have some seasickness medicine available.

Dos and don'ts: Do remember that landing is dependent on weather conditions, and shore excursions are only possible about 60 per cent of the time. Do come properly prepared for the extreme conditions, with warm, waterproof and windproof clothing. Don't forget binoculars.

Fierce winds and waves sculpt the icebergs of Antarctica into elaborate castle-like structures with turrets and arches.

the unspoilt interior, with its mountains and ancient forests. It is also the starting point for cruises to Antarctica.

The ship sails east from Ushuaia to the Falkland Islands (Las Malvinas to the Spanish-speaking world), 400 kilometres (250 miles) east of Argentina. The capital, Stanley, hugs a sheltered harbour in East Falkland, the largest island. A British Overseas Territory with red telephone boxes and traditional pubs, the islands are home to more than 200 species of migratory birds, as well as sea lions, penguins (including the rare rockhopper penguin), elephant seals and killer whales.

From the Falklands, the ship journeys southeast, often accompanied by a wandering albatross, which will follow ships in the hope of picking up scraps. This magnificent creature has the longest wing span of any bird, at up to 3.5 metres (11 ft). At the Antarctic Convergence (where warmer northern waters meet the cooler southern seas), the temperature drops markedly. This mingling of the waters produces an abundance of krill, a tiny crustacean which is the staple diet of many Antarctic species, and are rich hunting grounds for whales, seals, squid, icefish, penguins and albatrosses.

Christ Church Cathedral in Stanley, East Falkland, was built in 1892. The arch next to the cathedral was erected in 1933 to commemorate 100 years of British administration of the Falklands. It is made from the jawbones of two blue whales. The cathedral is shown here on a rare sunny day – it rains on more than 300 days a year in the Falkland Islands.

The next stop is South Georgia, a mountainous island permanently swathed in snow and ice. It is uninhabited but for the staff of the British Antarctic Survey. Visitors will be astonished by the magnificent sight of tens of thousands of king penguins, huddling around the rocky bays. There may be an opportunity to visit the grave of the Antarctic explorer Ernest Shackleton (1874–1922). The ship continues south through the Scotia Sea to the starkly beautiful South Orkney Islands. Glaciers edge into the grey waters, and moss and lichen carpet the stony slopes where penguins nest.

In 1916, Shackleton and his expedition team sought refuge on Elephant Island after their ship was destroyed by pack ice. Wind-whipped and frozen, it is rarely possible to land. The island is among the most northerly of the South Shetland Islands, a small archipelago lying 120 km (80 miles) off the Antarctic peninsula. Numerous species of seal and penguin thrive here. The half-moon curve of Deception Island is formed by a volcanic caldera, and provides one of the most sheltered bays in these parts. It is possible to hike to the crater rim to enjoy magnificent views over the island.

The sheet ice becomes denser and the icebergs ever more colossal as the ship presses on to Hope Bay on the Antarctic mainland, the ice creaking and groaning as it shifts in the petrol-grey seas. Hope Bay is dotted with the low-built edifices of international scientific research stations. At home in this blinding white landscape are seals, penguins and whales, while terns, petrels and cormorants wheel through the skies.

The return journey takes two days, negotiating the stormy Drake Passage. It rounds Cape Horn, and enters the calmer waters of the Beagle Channel, where Charles Darwin glimpsed his first glaciers in 1833, and which is named after his ship, the HMS *Beagle*. The voyage ends back at Ushuaia.

Many sea mammals and birds, such as the elephant seal (above), breed on South Georgia island. The animals' breeding grounds are protected, so ships are only allowed to berth at one place on the island – Grytviken.

THE ORIENT EXPRESS

Start London **End** Venice

Countries crossed UK, France, Liechtenstein, Austria, Switzerland, Italy

Distance 2,250 kilometres (1,400 miles)

Transport used Train

Highlights Sacre Coeur, Alpine scenery, Grand Canal, the Art Deco carriages

Forever associated with luxury, sophistication and – thanks to Agatha Christie – a hint of danger and mystery, the Orient Express is one of the world's most celebrated rail travel experiences. The first trips began in the 1880s, but the 1930s saw the zenith of the Orient Express routes, with three parallel services running: the Orient Express, the Simplon Orient Express and the Arlberg Orient Express. It extended from one edge of continental Europe to the other, reaching its farthest endpoint in Istanbul.

In the 1970s, the Compagnie Internationale des Wagons-Lits, which ran the Orient Express, stopped running carriages, but in 1982, American businessman James Sherwood set up the Venice-Simplon Express after buying 35 sleeper, restaurant and Pullman carriages. The Venice-Simplon Orient Express is a private luxury train service that travels primarily from London to Venice, but other routes are available on a more limited basis. By combining the London–Paris–Venice route with the special service from Venice to Istanbul, it is also possible to follow the original Orient Express route.

Luxury is the byword of the Orient Express experience. As you board the gleaming carriages of the British Pullman train at London Victoria station, a personal steward escorts you to your reserved seat. After crossing the channel, you board the blue and gold carriages of the Continental Orient Express trains, or Wagon-Lits. On reaching Paris, there is a pause of a few hours, giving you the chance to take a quick look around the city. The journey proper begins on re-boarding. Sipping a cocktail as you watch the countryside race past, there's time to anticipate the four-course dinner that will follow shortly. After dinner you can linger in the bar car, listening to the baby grand piano. When you are ready to retire to your cabin, you'll find it has been transformed into a cosy bedroom. As you sleep, the Orient Express is routed from Paris via Basel to Zurich, then through the Arlberg Pass to Innsbruck, through the Brenner Pass to Verona and on to Venice. On waking the next morning, you'll probably be approaching Zurich, with Swiss lakes outside your window when you put up the blind. Breakfast is delivered to your compartment by your steward.

The Grand Canal is one of the main waterways through Venice. It is a busy thoroughfare, with water buses, water taxis and gondolas vying for space. Lining the canal are buildings that date from the 13th to the 18th century, the period when the Republic of Venice was at the height of its power.

TRAVELLER'S TIPS

Best time to go: Avoid the winter months and high summer. April to June is ideal, as the continental climate is warm and dry during these months.

Look out for: The Arlberg Pass, the Brenner Pass, the Grand Canal, Rialto Bridge, Saint Mark's Basilica, the Doge's Palace.

Dos and don'ts: Do sit back, relax and enjoy the journey on the Orient Express. Don't forget to take smart clothes to wear when dressing for dinner.

Vaduz Castle, the seat of the princes of Liechtenstein, overlooks the tiny principality. German-speaking Liechtenstein is the only country to lie entirely within the Alps, and is surrounded by spectacular peaks.

The train cuts across the principality of Liechtenstein before crossing into Austria via the spectacularly scenic Arlberg Pass. The railway hugs the valley wall, snaking along the mountain sides, and after Innsbruck the train turns south through the equally scenic Brenner Pass into Italy to reach Verona. Turning east again, the train reaches Venice Mestre on the mainland, then rumbles slowly over the causeway, finally arriving at Venice Santa Lucia terminus on the shores of the Grand Canal in central Venice.

Venice is the capital of the region Veneto. Famous for its canals, it stretches across 117 small islands in the marshy Venetian Lagoon along the Adriatic Sea in northeast Italy. Venice is the world's only pedestrian city, is easily walkable, and the absence of cars makes it a particularly pleasant experience. The Rialtine islands – the 'main' part of Venice – are small enough to walk from one end to the other in about an hour. If you want to get around a bit more quickly, there are numerous water buses, known as *vaporetti*, and water taxis. If you want to have a romantic ride along the canals, take a gondola ride. St Mark's Basilica, with its magnificent Byzantine architecture, is located on the Piazza San Marco and is one of the highlights of a visit to Venice. Another must-see is the Doge's Palace, the seat of government of the former Venetian Republic. Don't miss the Rialto market – shopping there is slightly less expensive than in the tourist-filled Piazza San Marco – and the Rialto Bridge, on San Polo. The Rialto Bridge has become one of Venice's most recognizable icons, and has a history that spans over 800 years. After exploring the streets of Venice, there is the option to change trains and continue on to Istanbul. Alternatively, spend a couple of nights in Venice before returning home.

EL CAMINO DE SANTIAGO

Start St-Jean-Pied-de-Port **End** Santiago de Compostela
Countries crossed France, Spain
Distance 800 kilometres (500 miles) **Transport used** On foot
Highlights Pamplona, Estella-Lizarra, Burgos, León, Santiago de Compostela

According to medieval legend, one night in 813 AD a shepherd in Galicia was guided by a trail of stars to the burial place of St James, one of the 12 Apostles. The site – which became known as Santiago de Compostela ('St James of the Field of Stars') – soon became an important place of pilgrimage. By the 12th century, it was one of the most popular pilgrimages in Europe, with a system of hostels and shelters to feed and lodge the pilgrims. There has been an enormous resurgence of interest in the last few decades: approximately 200,000 pilgrims walked to Santiago de Compostela in 2010.

Although there are many possible routes, in recent years one section has proved the most popular. Known as *el camino francés* ('the French Way'), it departs from Saint-Jean-Pied-de-Port on the French side of the Pyrenees, crossing the mountains at Roncesvalles before continuing towards the great cathedral city of León and then west to Santiago de Compostela. This is only a fraction of the route undertaken by medieval pilgrims, who travelled from villages and towns across Europe, but it is still an arduous journey, crossing mountains and hot dusty plains, and can take months to complete. The cathedral offers a *compostela*, a certificate of completion, to pilgrims who finish the last 100 kilometres (62 miles) on foot, or 200 kilometres (124 miles) on bicycle.

The Cathedral of Santiago de Compostela was consecrated in 1128. Over the centuries, the building has been expanded, and the western façade, shown here, was added in the 18th century.

The Church of St Mary of Eunate in Navarre is an octagonal Romanesque building dating from the 12th century. It stands along the *camino* in open fields and may once have been used as a hostel for pilgrims.

The first day's hike across the mountains from Saint-Jean-Pied-de-Port to the Spanish village of Roncesvalles is one of the most demanding of the entire route. Charlemagne and his armies famously met defeat in 778 at the pass of Roncesvalles, but the quiet valley is now noted for its fine cheeses and a smattering of Romanesque churches. The walk continues south towards Pamplona, capital of Navarra and famous for its annual bull-running festival. The historic quarter, an atmospheric huddle of narrow streets and café-lined squares, is dominated by the 14th-century Gothic cathedral. From Pamplona, the *camino* winds through Romanesque towns such as Puente La Reina, with its six-arched medieval bridge, and enchanting Estella, with its churches and bridges of golden stone. Vineyards signal that you are entering the Rioja region. Burgos is one of the largest cities along the *camino*, with a marvellous 13th-century Gothic cathedral (inscribed on the UNESCO World Heritage List), and a pair of elegant medieval monasteries, including one that functioned as a royal pantheon. The 11th-century Romanesque church of San Martín de Tours in Frómista has exquisite carvings around the portals. From Burgos the route heads westwards across the huge, flat expanse of the Castilian plain. Here, the sprawling city of León is also crowned by a vast cathedral, known as the 'House of Light' for its stained glass windows dating from the 13th to the 16th centuries.

Ponferrada, with a Templar's castle, is the last major town before crossing the mountains into Galicia. The westernmost region of Spain, Galicia is often compared to Ireland, due to its Celtic heritage, damp climate and green hills. Sarria, a small town with fine churches, is the last point at which walkers hoping to earn the *compostela* can join the pilgrimage.

The culmination of the *camino* is Santiago de Compostela, an entrancing city of stone built on a hilltop. At its heart is the cathedral, where the relics of St James are kept in the crypt beneath the main altar. The central pillar of the main doorway, the magnificent 12th-century Portico da Gloria, has been worn down by the touch of millions of hands over the centuries. A pilgrim's mass is held at noon each day.

The way is marked by the sign of the scallop shell. The grooves that score the shell culminate in a single point in the base, representing the many paths that lead to Santiago de Compostela. Traditionally pilgrims have carried a scallop shell with them on their walks, using it as a utensil for drinking water from rivers and streams.

THE NORWEGIAN COAST

The western coast of Norway is gouged into a succession of dramatic fjords, with sheer cliffs plummeting into icy seas, and secret valleys scored with waterfalls. This is a classic loop around the region, beginning in the historic town of Bergen, and heading up into the mountains on two of Europe's most scenic railways. A sail through the most beautiful fjord in Norway is followed by a thrilling drive up the twists and turns of Stalheim's Road. There are many opportunities for adventure tourism, with facilities for mountain-biking, salmon-fishing and whitewater rafting.

Beautiful Bergen is splayed along a jagged coastline, ringed by seven steep mountains, and overlooking the majestic Byfjorden fjord. Timber-clad houses climb up forested slopes, where cable cars sway up to the peaks for staggering views. Bergen was established in the 11th century, and rapidly developed into an important trading city largely thanks to its thriving cod-fishing industry. It was a powerful member of the Hanseatic League (an economic alliance of northern European trading cities and guilds). The old quarter (Byrggen) still preserves the original Hanseatic wharf, with its brightly coloured wooden warehouses. One of the oldest surviving timber buildings now contains an excellent museum dedicated to the history of the Hanseatic League. Bryggen still boasts narrow, cobbled streets lined with whitewashed wooden dwellings, most of which now contain shops, restaurants and cafés. Another of Byrggen's museums, built on the site of Bergen's first settlement, displays 800-year-old ruins and exhibits medieval tools and pottery. Near the harbour, the pungent Torgat fish market is an amazing spectacle, with all manner of aquatic creatures displayed on the ice-covered stalls.

The hour-long rail journey from Bergen to the lakeside town of Voss threads along the bank of the fjords, then into the mountains, crossing rivers and streams, and chugging past traditional farmsteads with their red-painted barns. Voss is a delightfully old-fashioned town set amid woods on the shores of a lake. The town has become increasingly well known for the adventurous activities on offer in its environs, which include whitewater rafting, salmon-fishing and mountain-

Bryggen (Norwegian for 'Wharf') is a series of beautifully preserved Hanseatic commercial buildings in Bergen. These are the oldest buildings in the city, and about a quarter date back to before 1702, when many of the warehouses in the area burned down in a fire.

biking. There are also two ski stations nearby. Voss is proud of its country cuisine, and many restaurant menus feature classic dishes such as *smalahove* – grilled sheep's head.

The train climbs east of Voss to the mountain station of Myrdal, which sits at 867 metres (2,844 ft) above sea level, and is the upper terminus of the celebrated Flåm railway. Built in the 1920s to link the main Bergen railway line with Flåm, a village on Norway's biggest fjord, Sognefjord, the Flåm Railway is one of the steepest rail lines in the world. It makes its 20-kilometre (12-mile) descent through breathtaking mountain scenery, passing rivers, ravines and snow-capped peaks, and pausing by dramatic waterfalls including the 93-metre (305-ft)-high Kjosfossen waterfall.

After exploring the village of Flåm at the inner end of the Aurlandsfjord (an arm of Sognefjord), take a boat out onto the fjords to see the sheer cliffs and wildlife at close quarters. With luck, you'll spot a seal peeking its head above the waters or eagles circling high overhead. Occasionally, you'll spot the vestiges of a clifftop farmstead, long abandoned. The Aurlandsfjord and Nærøyfjord are the most spectacular branches of the Sognefjord. Nærøyfjord's pristine beauty has earned it a place on Unesco's World Heritage List.

From Gudvangen, the Stalheimskleiva ('Stalheim's Road'), one of Europe's steepest and most panoramic roads, begins its exhilarating climb into the mountains. The road twists sharply through 13 hairpin bends, flanked on one side by the dramatic Stalheim Waterfall and on the other by the Sivle Waterfall. At the top, the Stalheim Hotel commands astonishing views. The road joins the main highway through this region, which will eventually bring you back to lakeside Voss, where trains depart regularly for Bergen.

Stalheim's Road zig-zags up the Stalheim Gorge, flanked on either side by spectacular waterfalls. At the top, during the summer months you can stay in the historic 19th-century Stalheim Hotel.

TRAVELLER'S TIPS

Best time to go: June and July are the most popular months to travel, thanks to the long days around the summer solstice. To avoid the crowds, visit in May or September. For skiing and winter sports, come between December and February.

Look out for: Although it is difficult to see the Aurora Borealis below the Arctic Circle, you may be lucky and see the Northern Lights.

Dos and don'ts: Don't drink and drive: Norway's laws are among the strictest in Europe. Do book activities and rail excursions in advance to avoid disappointment.

THE TRANS-PYRENEAN ROUTE

San Sebastián
Hondarribia
Parque Nacional de Ordesa y Monte Perdido
Cadaqués
Parc Nacional d'Aigüestortes
Cap de Creus

Start Cadaqués **End** Hondarribia

Countries crossed Spain and France

Distance 830 kilometres (516 miles) **Transport used** On foot

Highlights Cadaqués, Cap de Creus, Parc Nacional d'Aigüestortes, Parque Nacional de Ordesa y Monte Perdido, Hondarribia, wildlife, birding

Part of an extensive network of trails, tracks and paths, the GR11 traverses the Spanish Pyrenees, from the wild headland of the Cap de Creus on the Mediterranean Sea to the elegant Basque port of Hondarribia on the Atlantic Coast. The trail takes between four to six weeks to complete, and wends its way through towering peaks, verdant meadows and traditional villages and towns. Although few sections require technical mountaineering skills, this trail is demanding and is suitable only for seasoned hikers.

The immaculate white town of Cadaqués crowns the western tip of the Cap de Creus as it juts into the Mediterranean. It is a wild and rugged headland imbued with a special quality of light that has inspired the many artists who have visited the town, including Pablo Picasso, Joan Miró and Salvador Dalí. Dalí liked the area so much that he made his home in a whitewashed fisherman's cottage in Port Lligat, which adjoins Cadaqués, overlooking an idyllic, island-flecked bay. From here, the trail skirts the northern flanks of the headland, passing the lofty and remote Monastery of Sant Pere near Port de la Selva and then striking north. As it enters the Catalan Pyrenees, the GR11 crosses the National Park of Aigüestortes ('twisted waters' in Catalan), a spellbinding wilderness encompassing sheer crags of granite and slate and glacial lakes. Here, rivers teeming with brown trout course through dense forests, creating glittering waterfalls and shimmering natural pools. Across the border into Aragón, the trail enters another breathtaking nature reserve, the Parque Nacional de Ordesa y Monte Perdido, where lammergeiers and eagles

The peaks of the Pyrenees form a natural border between France and Spain. While the region is popular with skiers in the winter months, many parts have been set aside as conservation areas to preserve the flora and fauna.

With a wingspan approaching 3 metres (10 ft), the Eurasian Griffon vulture is at home among the towering peaks of the Pyrenees. Tens of thousands of the birds can be found in the mountains running from the Mediterranean to the Atlantic.

wheel lazily in the thermals overhead, while chamois, marmot and boar scrabble around on the mountainsides below. One of the highlights of the trek is an ascent of Monte Perdido ('Lost Mountain'), which at 3,355 metres (11,007 ft), is the third highest peak in the Pyrenees. Beyond this, lies the Valle de Vallibierna, a region scored with deep gullies and canyons, including one which plunges for 200 metres (650 ft). This area is one of the most scarcely populated, and walkers should ensure that they have adequate supplies to last for several days.

Continuing east, highlights of the second part of the GR11 trail include the forest of Irati, which is split between Navarra and the Basque lands. These dense forests are scattered with lakes, and the shaded paths make for exceptional walking. Farther on, the Baztán Valley is dotted with ancient villages, with traditional stone houses and picturesque Romanesque

churches. Marmots, wild boar and mountain deer are regularly spotted in the surrounding hills. However, it is extremely unlikely you'll catch a glimpse of the very rare Pyrenean bear, as there are believed to be fewer than 20 in the region, despite a programme to reintroduce them to the mountains. Heading west into the Basque lands, there is a series of arduous ascents and descents, but the views over the valleys are breathtaking and well worth the effort of the climbs.

Finally, the trail descends towards the charming harbour town of Hondarribia, sitting on the border between France and Spain at the mouth of the River Bidasoa. The town contains a castle and ancient fortified walls, which stand as a testament to the battles fought in the area between the 16th and 18th centuries. The brightly painted houses, whose balconies are filled with flowers, overlook an atmospheric fishing port. With

the backdrop of the Jaizkibel Mountains, the town itself sits on a small promontory, looking over the Txingudi Bay to the French town of Hendaye on the other side. A short excursion leads to the Cabo Higuer, lying at the western end of the GR11 trail. This marks the northeasternmost corner of Spain, and a visit here is rewarded by the chance to watch the stunning sunset over the bay.

The eerie ruins of Peyrepertuse Castle in the French Pyrenees are all that remain of a haven and mountain stronghold of the Cathars, a Christian sect that flourished in the 12th and 13th centuries before being suppressed by the Church.

THE ROMANTIC ROAD

Start Würzburg **End** Füssen	
Countries crossed Germany	
Distance 350 kilometres (220 miles)	
Transport used Car	
Highlights Würzburg, Dinkelsbühl, Augsburg, Landsberg am Lech, Neuschwanstein Castle	

The Romantic Road winds through pristine valleys scattered with perfectly preserved medieval towns and villages, past vineyards and pastures, and into the foothills of the Bavarian Alps. Castles, palaces and monasteries beckon, and a wealth of nature reserves provide respite from the crowds.

The immaculate little city of Würzburg is the starting point of the Romantic Road, a suitably fairytale vision crowned with a mighty fortress and a lavish 18th-century palace. The Fortress Marienberg is built over the ruins of a 3,000-year-old Celtic citadel. The heart of the old town is the splendid Marktplatz ('Market Square'), flanked with gabled houses and overlooked by the Gothic Marienkapelle. From there, a mesh of narrow streets fan out, lined with lively bars and restaurants. Würzburg was long ruled by the prince-archbishops of the Shönborn dynasty, notably Balthazar Neumann, who ordered the construction of the 'palace of palaces', a dizzying Baroque concoction built between 1719 and 1744. The Venetian painter Tiepolo (1696–1770) was commissioned to create the enormous fresco – still the largest painting in the world – which spreads magnificently over the main staircase.

Drive on past Tauberbischofsheim, with its half-timbered houses and continue along the beautiful valley to Rothenburg, which sits serenely on the banks of the River Tauber. An enchanting little city of red-roofed houses and graceful squares, this perfect time capsule has featured in several films, including *Chitty Chitty Bang Bang* and *Harry Potter and the Deathly Hallows*.

Like Rothenburg, Dinkelsbühl to the south is still circled by its medieval walls, studded with 16 towers. Its neighbour, Nördlingen, is the third in the group to have retained its fortifications almost completely intact. Continue south to handsome Augsburg, one of the grandest cities on the Romantic Road. It developed from a Roman settlement, which was strategically located at the crux of several important

Neuschwanstein Castle was built for Bavarian king Ludwig II. Perched on a hill overlooking the village of Hohenschwangau, the castle has been open to the public ever since Ludwig's death in 1886.

trade routes. It grew increasingly prosperous, reaching the apogee of its power in the 15th and 16th centuries, when affluent merchants funded the construction of a wealth of handsome churches and palaces. The Thirty Years War (1618–48) put an end to the city's Golden Age, and Augsburg entered a slow decline. Centuries of benign neglect preserved the old city in aspic, and today it is a charming university city replete with excellent museums and galleries.

Füssen, at the southern end of the Romantic Road, sits in the foothills of the Alps a few kilometres from the border with Austria. Many scenes for the film *The Great Escape* were filmed in and around the town, including Steve McQueen's famous motorcycle stunts.

Landsberg am Lech is another storybook town, which sits on the banks of the River Lech and is encircled by magnificent gates and towers. Founded in the 13th century, the old quarter is dominated by the sumptuous city hall with lavish stucco decoration. The narrow lanes are lined by a wealth of fine churches and elegantly restored Renaissance townhouses. The Bavarian Gate, a superb Gothic portal, is the finest surviving gateway, and stands testament to the town's historic importance. Just outside the old city, a beautiful park adorns the river banks, perfect for picnics and languid strolls.

The road meanders through the Pfaffenwinkel ('Parson's Corner'), a bucolic landscape of rolling hills and pasture land dotted with minuscule villages and beautiful churches. Finest of these is the Wieskirche Pilgrimage Church, with a superb rococo interior, which is now a UNESCO World Heritage

Site and regularly features classical concerts. The scenery becomes increasingly rugged as it approaches the Bavarian Alps, where Neuschwanstein Castle appears like a mirage, perched high on a pale crag surrounded by dense forest. A Romantic fantasy in stone, the castle was commissioned by King Ludwig II, an eccentric known as 'Ludwig the Mad' who ruled Bavaria from 1864 to 1886, when he was deposed. Ludwig conceived a castle that would be a fitting dwelling place for the knight Lohengrin, a medieval knight of legend, who was eulogized in the eponymous opera by Richard Wagner, Ludwig's protegé. Murals depicting events from medieval epics decorate the grand salons, and Ludwig ensured that a special theatre was constructed where Wagner could stage his works. Unfortunately for poor Ludwig, he was found drowned in the castle lake before his project reached fruition, and he never saw the castle complete.

The expense of building drained the royal finances to such an extent that the castle was almost immediately opened to the public as a visitor attraction, and it is now one of the biggest attractions in Bavaria.

Nearby, little Füssen is tucked into a fold in the mountains. This is Bavaria's highest town, and contains a perfectly preserved medieval core replete with exquisite churches, mansions and palaces. It is crowned by a trio of spectacular monuments, built high above the town: a Gothic church and monastery of St Mang, and a superb summer palace, the Hohes Schloss, built for the prince bishops of Augsburg. The Romantic Road culminates in this picturesque town, but you can extend the trip a little further to climb Germany's highest peak, the 2,964-metre (9,724-ft) Zugspitze. From here, the views stretch across the Alps as far as Italy and Switzerland.

Nicknamed the 'Pearl of France', the town of Menton sits on the French-Italian border. As well as its idyllic harbour, Menton has half a dozen beaches, which prove popular with travellers touring along the French Riviera.

THE CORNICHES

Start Nice End Nice Countries crossed France
Distance 75 kilometres (47 miles) Transport used Car
Highlights Menton, Monaco, Villefranche-sur-Mer, Èze, Roquebrune, Cap Martin, La Turbie, Nice

The Côte d'Azur, a sparkling stretch of rugged Mediterranean coastline, has been immortalized by painters, poets, novelists and screenwriters. Heading east from Nice to the Italian border at Menton, three twisting roads hug the glamorous coast, spinning past millionaires' mansions and medieval villages, glossy casinos and harbours full of fishing boats. These roads, known as Les Trois Corniches, run roughly parallel to each other along the coastline, but each offers something different. The Grande Corniche is the highest of the three roads, with the most rewarding views. The Moyenne ('Middle') Corniche connects exquisite hilltop villages like Èze and Roquebrune, while the Basse ('Low') Corniche wriggles along the coastline, linking resorts, fishing villages and harbours. The route described here heads east along the Basse Corniche, and returns along the thrilling Grande Corniche: for more driving and less sightseeing, head to Menton along the panoramic Moyenne Corniche.

Nice is a lively, handsome city that has managed to escape the over-prettified fate of many Provençal towns. It has a beautifully restored old quarter, famous for its colourful flower market, and wonderful

The narrow, medieval streets of Èze twist and meander through the ancient town, flanked on either side by old buildings, which now house craft shops, art galleries and museums.

pebbly beaches backed by grand 19th-century hotels. East of Nice, the seaside resort of Villefranche-sur-Mer boasts fine sand beaches and a charming fishermen's quarter, where a tiny chapel painted by Jean Cocteau sits near the port. Beyond it, the Cap Ferrat peninsula boasts beautiful coastal paths out to the lighthouse at its tip, and contains several lavish homes belonging to aristocrats and millionaires. One such mansion, the Villa Ephrussi de Rothschild, is now a museum, filled with antiques and paintings, and surrounded by gardens.

Beaulieu-Sur-Mer is another smart seaside resort, with a huge yacht harbour and another magnificent museum located in a historic residence built between 1902 and 1906 for the banker and collector Théodore Reinach. The Greek-style Villa Kérylos has a stunning location right on the water's edge, and is filled with artworks from ancient Greece.

Past the promontory of Cap d'Ail, dotted with millionaires' mansions, you'll arrive in bright, brash Monaco. This tiny principality is a mini-Manhattan of glamorous apartment blocks, with Monte Carlo at its heart. Beyond Monaco is another enclave of luxurious residences, Cap Martin, and behind it on a hilltop is the enchanting medieval village of Roquebrune. The castle, called the Château des Grimaldis after its earliest rulers, was begun in the 12th century, and its keep is the oldest in France. Roquebrune's narrow streets, with their covered passages and ancient stone houses, are a delight to wander, and the main square offers extraordinary views out across the azure sea.

Menton, a lovely old city in shades of ochre and yellow, is famous for its citrus orchards, which fill the air with the scent of their blossom in early spring. The old city is a tumble of red-tiled rooftops spilling down the hill, while the waterfront is backed by

grand 19th-century hotels and mansions. There are several luxuriant gardens, including the Maria Serena and the Val Rahmeh gardens, both laid out at the turn of the 20th century. Jean Cocteau decorated the Salle de Mariages in the City Hall, and he is remembered in an excellent museum.

The return journey will take you along the upper reaches of the mountains that define this stretch of coast. The views are extraordinary, not just of the mythical coastline but also back towards the Alpine peaks in the distance. The Grande Corniche was constructed by Napoleon in 1806, but follows the route of the Roman Via Aurelia which once linked Rome with the Iberian peninsula. Hilltop La Turbie is dominated by the massive remains of a Roman monument, La Trophée des Alpes, which was erected to celebrate the defeat of Ligurian tribes in the region in 7 BC.

The 19th-century casino, built in the distinctive beaux-arts style, lies at the heart of Monte Carlo. As well as the world-famous casino, the building complex houses an opera and a ballet house. In 1873, the casino attracted great publicity when Joseph Jagger, an English engineer, discovered a bias in one of the roulette tables and 'broke the bank of Monte Carlo'.

Èze is the only village along this route that connects all three of the Corniche roads. A picturesque medieval village, it sits high on a well-fortified hilltop with far-reaching views of the coast: it is easy to see why it was nicknamed the 'eagle's nest' in medieval times. The cobbled streets culminate in the lofty château, now a luxurious hotel and restaurant. From here, the road dips as it reaches Nice, passing a 19th-century observatory with a dome designed by Gustave Eiffel, and then enters the city near its harbour.

THE SPINE OF CORSICA

Start Calenzana **End** Conca

Countries crossed France

Distance 180 kilometres (110 miles)

Transport used On foot

Highlights Cirque de la Solitude, Lac de Nino, Lac de Melo, Lac de Capitello, ascent of Monte Cinto, Aiguilles de Bavella

Almost two-thirds of Corsica is covered by mountains, and the GR20 hiking trail traverses the highest peaks along the island's spine. The trek takes approximately two weeks, and encompasses an incredible variety of terrain, from the verdant slopes of the Balagne in the north to the jagged crags of the Alta Rocca in the south. On the way it passes glacial lakes, maquis, bogs, rock pools and waterfalls, home to the elusive mouflon (wild sheep) and the enormous bearded vulture.

section, but also the most spectacular. The northern trailhead is Calenzana, a village set amid farms and olive groves. Highlights of this northern section include the footbridge at Spasimata, which is suspended above limpid rock pools and a small waterfall, and most notably the Cirque de la Solitude. This is a difficult crossing for the average hiker, and requires the aid of ladders and ropes bolted into the sheer rock face. The optional ascent of Monte Cinto (2,706m/8,878ft), Corsica's highest peak, is a challenge few experienced mountaineers will be able to resist. The Lac de Nino, a deep blue glacial lake, is backed by pale crags and surrounded by lush, green meadows where semi-wild mountain horses graze in summer.

More inviting glacial lakes await on the southern section of the walk, including the Lac de Melo and the Lac de Capitello. The icy waters are invigorating after an arduous climb. Other highlights of the southern section include two of the highest peaks, the Monte d'Oro and the Monte Incudine, which are particularly demanding ascents but offer sweeping vistas as a reward. Perhaps the most iconic image of the GR20 is the surreal ridge of jagged rocks pointing at the sky in the Alta Rocca region. The Aiguilles de Bavella ('Bavella Needles') are located near the culmination of the trail, at the village of Conca just north of Porto Vecchio on Corsica's southeastern coast.

The trail is divided into two sections, north and south, which are linked at the town of Vizzavona, where there are transport links to the coast. Although it can be hiked in either direction, most people begin in the north, which is the most demanding

The Aiguilles de Bavella in southern Corsica rise to a height of more than 1,600 metres (5,250 ft). As the sun moves across the sky, the colour of these rocky spires changes from deep ochre to a shiny golden yellow.

TRAVELLER'S TIPS

Best time to go: The best time to hike the trail is in June or September, avoiding the heat and crush of July and August (the most popular months).

Look out for: Keep the red and white painted markings of the trail in sight to avoid losing the path; don't rely on the stone cairns.

Dos and don'ts: Do book accommodation in the gites or refuges along the trail in advance; this is now obligatory.

THE SKY ROAD

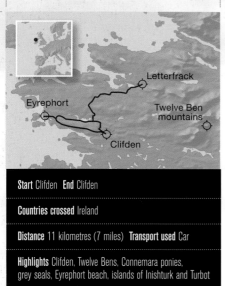

Letterfrack

Eyrephort

Twelve Ben mountains

Clifden

Start Clifden **End** Clifden

Countries crossed Ireland

Distance 11 kilometres (7 miles) **Transport used** Car

Highlights Clifden, Twelve Bens, Connemara ponies, grey seals, Eyrephort beach, islands of Inishturk and Turbot

The Maumturk mountains mark the boundary between Connemara and the rest of County Galway.

Connemara occupies a broad peninsula in western Ireland and encapsulates the best of traditional Ireland. The landscape is spellbinding, encompassing dramatic mountains and undulating coastline, bogs and loughs, mist-covered hills and emerald-green fields. There are few large towns, just a scattering of farms and traditional villages, where Gaelic is still the predominant language. The Sky Road is the region's most scenic drive, a circular route that loops around a remote headland dotted with islands.

Begin in Clifden, a handsome little town half lost in the folds of the green hills. It was founded by local landowner John D'Arcy, whose ruined castle now stands on the outskirts of the town. Thanks to its location on the most westerly tip of Europe, Clifden was chosen as the site for one of the earliest transatlantic wireless telegraphy stations, which sent messages to its sister station in eastern Canada between 1907 and 1911. British aviators Alcock and Brown completed the first transatlantic flight here in 1919, when they crashlanded into Derrygimlagh bog south of the town. Behind Clifden is the singular silhouette of the Twelve Bens ('Beanna Beola' in Gaelic), a ridge of small, sharp-peaked mountains that are a popular destination for hill-walkers.

The Sky Road is well signposted, heading west out of town, and passing the ruins of Clifden Castle. Erected by D'Arcy in 1750, the castle was once the finest estate in these parts, built in the Gothic Revival style and surrounded by elegant gardens. Abandoned little more than a century later, it fell into ruins and the park reverted to wilderness, but now it makes for a romantic wander.

TRAVELLER'S **TIPS**

Best time to go: Come in May, June or September to avoid the summer crowds. October and November can be good months to visit, with beautiful autumn light.

Look out for: There are great local festivals in April and September if you are interested in traditional arts and music. Activities available in the region include sailing, horse-riding, cycling and fishing.

Dos and don'ts: Do pack waterproofs, even if visiting in summer.

Just beyond the castle, the Sky Road splits briefly into two. The upper road is the most popular thanks to its far-reaching views, while the lower road hugs the coastline closely. The upper road climbs ever higher, passing an old coastguard station, offering increasingly dramatic views as it approaches the summit of the peninsula. There's a lookout point right at the very top, which offers stunning views in all directions. From here, you can gaze out over the offshore islands of Inishturk (meaning 'wild boar') and Turbot, and perhaps glimpse dolphins or grey seals. (There is no regular ferry service to the islands, but a local tour company arranges guided walks, which include boat transport.) The road continues north, past whitewashed cottages and green fields

where the Connemara ponies graze peacefully. The breed, known for their intelligence, hardiness and versatility, is now reared across the world.

A short detour off the Sky Road will bring you to the hamlet of Eyrephort at the tip of the peninsula, site of the only known Viking burial in Galway. Here, you'll find tiny coves and beaches of fine sand enclosed by black rocks. Back on the Sky Road, a megalithic portal tomb has survived for more than 5,000 years at Knockavally, the next hamlet along the route. The road curves around the narrow inlet of Streamstown Bay, passing a quarry that produces Connemara marble – a dark mossy shade of green. It has

The origin of Connemara's ponies, world-renowned for their hardiness, is unclear. They may have been brought to the region by the Vikings, but some believe that they arrived with the Andalusians who came ashore here after the Spanish Armada was wrecked off the Irish coast in 1588.

been a valuable commodity since the earliest settlers occupied these shores thousands of years ago, and remains a sought-after and expensive material.

The Sky Road meets the N59, the main local highway, where it returns south towards Clifden. But it's well worth extending the journey by turning north to Letterfrack, just 15 kilometres (9 miles) north of Clifden, where the visitors' centre for the Connemara National Park is located. This wild and beautiful nature reserve is a paradise for walkers and bird-watchers, with several trails exploring the region's bogs, heaths, grasslands and quiet woods. The park is particularly rich in songbirds – including meadow pipits, skylarks, stonechats,

The sun rises over Lough Derryclare, with the Twelve Bens Mountains behind it. The lough is 8 kilometres (5 miles) long, and is a popular destination for fishermen, offering salmon, grilse and trout.

robins and wrens – and even runs special 'dawn chorus' tours to hear them at their finest. The park also incorporates several peaks of the Twelve Bens range. Much of the land now protected in the reserve originally belonged to Kylemore Abbey, established in the 1920s on the grounds of an earlier castle, which enjoys a stunning location on the shores of a lough. The Abbey and its restored Victorian gardens can also be visited from Letterfrack.

ANDALUCÍA'S WHITE VILLAGES

Start Arcos de la Frontera **End** Castellar de la Frontera

Countries crossed Spain

Distance 300 kilometres (200 miles)

Transport used Car

Highlights Arcos de la Frontera, Sierra de Grazalema, Ronda, pueblos blancos ('white villages'), Sierra de Alcornales, wildlife, birdwatching

This driving tour sweeps around the mountainous hinterland of southern Andalucía, visiting the gleaming whitewashed villages bequeathed by the Arabs, and admiring the sturdy castles and lavish churches built after the armies of the Reconquista ('Reconquest') had regained control of the region in the 13th century. There are several magnificent natural parks to explore, with superb hiking trails and opportunities for birdwatching and other activities.

Arcos de la Frontera, set on the very edge of a sheer cliff above the River Guadalete, is the most striking of the 'white villages' in this region. The most celebrated landmark is the Gothic basilica of Santa María, erected over the great mosque in the 13th century. The basilica's belltower contains ten bells that, according to legend, sounded throughout the war with the Moors.

Head north from Arcos de la Frontera to Espera, an ancient town still dominated by the ruins of an Arab fortress, and then drop down east along a winding minor road to Bornos, which sits on the shores of a lake. Herons and ospreys nest by the lake, and otters swim in its waters. The historic quarter of sleepy agricultural Villamartín boasts several fine palaces and townhouses, and, on the road to Prado del Rey, the overgrown ruins of a ninth-century Arab fortress occupy a lonely hilltop. Prado del Rey itself is handsomely set against a mountainous backdrop, and was the site of the Roman settlement of Iptuci.

El Bosque is the gateway to the Parque Natural Sierra de Grazalema, an unspoilt landscape of limestone cliffs carpeted in Mediterreanean forest. Ubrique to the south has been famous for its leather goods since Arabic times, but its history stretches all the way back to the Phoenicians. Now a large city, it sits at the foot of the Sierra de Ubrique.

Tiny Benaocaz boasts a handsome Baroque town hall and a Renaissance church, and just beyond it, Villaluenga del Rosario is famous for its astonishing bullring, gouged out of the rock. Tiny whitewashed Grazalema is a perfect base for exploring the surrounding natural park of the same name. A twisting road leads to Zahara de la Sierra.

Curving past the shores of a small lake, the road comes to Algodonales, set amid olive groves and orchards in the foothills of the Sierra de Líjar. There are many activities in the region, including hiking, birdwatching and gliding. Olvera is piled up on a hilltop, magnificently crowned by the Church of Nuestra Señora de la Encarnación, surrounded by olive groves. Ronda is a breathtaking city straddling a steep gorge.

Zahara de la Sierra sits at the foot of a rocky outcrop topped by the ruins of a Moorish castle. It overlooks a manmade lake formed by a dam that must be crossed to enter the town.

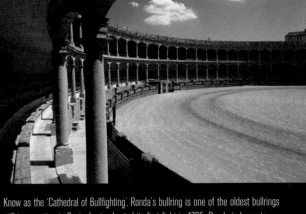

Know as the 'Cathedral of Bullfighting', Ronda's bullring is one of the oldest bullrings still in operation in Spain, having hosted its first fight in 1785. Ronda is home to several famous bullfighting dynasties, including the Romeros – three generations of Toreadors who were important figures in the development of bullfighting.

'Old' Ronda is a delicious little maze, replete with grand palaces (some of which are now museums) and full of miniature alleys and secret squares. The 'new' city – laid out in the 18th and 19th centuries – is best known for its bullring. The nearby villages of Benaoján and Montejaque are surrounded by cliffs pocked with caves that were inhabited in paleolithic times. More evidence of early settlement survives at Jimera de Líbar, where a Phoenician necropolis has been discovered. There are more Arabic castles to be discovered in Atajate and Benadalid, which both enjoy tranquil rural settings amid the mountains.

Lofty Gaucín, clustered at the foot of another castle-topped crag, is famous for its spectacular views over the Costa del Sol and the mountainous hinterland. Casares, a little closer to the coast, is a picturesque huddle of whitewashed cubes beneath a medieval tower.

Turn back inland to find Jimena de la Frontera on the fringes of the Parque Natural de los Alcornocales, a blissful wilderness which shelters some of the most extensive Mediterranean cork forest on the Iberian peninsula. The town's steep, cobbled streets culminate in the castle ruins, which afford far-reaching views out across the hills.

The journey culminates in Castellar de la Frontera, a spectacular fortified town still ringed by medieval walls. The village had been largely abandoned a couple of decades ago, but substantial investment and restoration have seen its fortunes revive.

The Puente Nuevo ('New Bridge') spans the 120-metre (390-ft)-deep El Tajo gorge, and connects the old quarter of the city of Ronda to the new. The bridge took 42 years to build and was completed in 1751.

THE GRANDES ALPES ROUTE

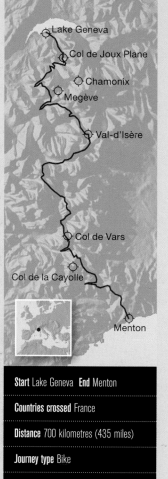

Lake Geneva
Col de Joux Plane
Chamonix
Megève
Val-d'Isère
Col de Vars
Col de la Cayolle
Menton

Start Lake Geneva **End** Menton

Countries crossed France

Distance 700 kilometres (435 miles)

Journey type Bike

Highlights Alpine scenery, sixteen 'cols' which feature on the Tour de France, Lake Geneva, Briançon, Bonneval-sur-Arc, St Martin-Vésubie, Menton

The Route des Grandes Alpes, a panoramic road through the remote peaks of the French Alps, was conceived in the first decades of the 20th century to promote the newly popular automobile. The road was completed in 1937 and is now a superb cycling route, which runs from Lake Geneva to the Mediterranean through majestic Alpine scenery and over sixteen iconic 'cols' or mountains passes.

The starting point is Thonon-les-Bains, sprawled along the southern shore of Lake Geneva (Lac Léman in French). The road winds through green valleys, canyons and the ruins of Aulps Abbey, an important Cistercian monastery. There is a climb through Alpine meadows and over the Col de la Colombière at 1,613 metres (5,292 ft). The Col des Aravis at 1,486 metres (4,875 ft) is overlooked by a tiny stone chapel dedicated to Saint Anne, where travellers once prayed for a safe passage across the mountains. Beyond the handsome town of Beaufort, nestled in a green valley and famous for its cheese, another long, steep climb begins. There are wonderful views of the turquoise waters of the Reservoir de Roselend from the Col de Meraillet at 1,605 metres (5,266 ft), but the highest point is the Cormet de Roselend at 1,968 metres (6,457 ft).

From Bourg-Saint-Maurice, the route borders the Parc National de la Vanoise, France's first national park. The road begins to climb, heading towards a clutch of ski resorts including Val d'Isère. After a gruelling, zig-zag ascent, you'll cross the highest pass in France, the Col de l'Iseran, at 2,770 metres (9,090 ft), which offers staggering views. Beyond it, the alluring Alpine town of Bonneval-sur-Arc, the highest village in France, is the perfect place to sit and recuperate.

The mighty peak of Mont Blanc, the highest point in the Alps, is visible from the shores of Lake Geneva, the starting point for this journey.

TRAVELLER'S **TIPS**

Best time to go: The route can be cycled from early June to October, but is best tackled during the long days of June and July.

Look out for: The trail reaches an altitude of 2,770 metres (9,090 ft), so dress accordingly. Pick up a map for date-stamping from the Grande Traversée des Alpes.

Dos and don'ts: Do train thoroughly: this route is physically demanding. Do check that the cols are open in advance.

During the summer months, the snow-free peaks of the Col de Vars reflect in the still waters of a mountain lake. This challenging route has been part of the Tour de France more than 30 times.

The longest ascent follows the town of Lanselbourg and the Col du Télégraphe. This is a demanding route up to the mythical Col du Galibier at 2,645 metres (8,678 ft). It was first included on the Tour de France in 1911 and has featured many times since. This is followed by a welcome descent down to the fortified 17th-century town of Briançon, which is set amid a ring of rugged peaks. Heading south from Briançon, another steep climb awaits: the road twists and turns its way through sharp hairpin curves to the Col d'Izoard at 2,361 metres (7,746 ft). There are few trees for shade and the landscape becomes increasingly barren as it winds around the Casse Deserte, a vast scree bowl dotted with jagged rocks.

The Col de Vars at 2,108 metres (6,916 ft) is the next challenge and it presents another stiff zig-zag ascent. A few kilometres beyond it, the immense Fort de Tournoux was built into the cliff face between 1843 and 1900 in order to defend France's eastern boundary. Farther south lies the pretty town of Barcelonnette, strung out along a river bank, after which there is a steep climb past scenic gorges and wooded valleys to the Col de la Cayolle at 2,326 metres (7,631 ft). A narrow descent swings past the villages of St Martin d'Entraunes and Guillaumes, before the route begins to rise once again to cross the Col de Valberg at 1,673 metres (5,489 ft). Beyond the Col de la Couillole at 1,678 metres (5,505 ft), there's a majestic descent down a beautiful mountain valley towards the delightful little village of St Sauveur. The next stage of the route twists up towards the Col St Martin at 1,500 metres (4,921 ft), before reaching the most southerly ski resort in the Alps, La Colmaine. Then it's a quick drop down to St Martin-Vésubie, with its cobbled streets piled steeply around a crag in the Mercantour mountains.

The road then winds through the Col de Turini at 1,604 metres (5,262 ft) on its way south to Sospel. This is a charming town, with a well-kept historic centre. Beyond it, the scenery changes from verdant Alpine pastures to the arid, brush-covered slopes that herald the Mediterranean. The Col de Castillon at 707 metres (2,320 ft) is the last pass of the route, and the first to offer sparkling sea views. It's an easy descent over the last few kilometres before reaching the graceful seaside town of Menton, perched on the shores of the French Mediterranean.

The Pont-Vieux crosses the River Bevera in the town of Sospel. This toll bridge was built in the 13th century and has been beautifully preserved, despite being bombed by the Germans during the Second World War.

THE WESER RENAISSANCE ROUTE

Start Hannoversch Münden **End** Bremen

Countries crossed Germany

Distance 400 kilometres (250 miles)

Transport used Car

Highlights Hannoversch Münden, Einbeck, Höxter, Paderborn, Hameln, Lemgo, Minden and Bremen

The towns and villages along the Weser River are filled with magnificent buildings built in the 16th and early 17th centuries when the region was enjoying a cultural and economic boom. They were built in an architectural style now known as the Weser Renaissance, a regional interpretation of Renaissance forms. The Weser Renaissance Route, a drive from Hannoversch Münden to Bremen in northern Germany, links a string of towns along the Weser Valley.

The route begins at Hannoversch Münden, known locally simply as Münden, where the splendid city hall, with a trio of stepped gables, presides over the main square. A restrained castle, also from the early 17th century, sits near the river, which is crossed by one of the oldest stone bridges in Germany.

Upriver, Einbeck is another charming and well preserved town, famous for its brewery – one of the oldest in Europe. The enchanting little town of Höxter seems to have stepped from the pages of a fairy tale, with its half-timbered houses, and narrow lanes. Its finest monuments in the Weser Renaissance style are the old Deacon's House, with a remarkable façade studded with gilded rosettes, and the Adam-and-Eve house which lives up to its storybook name.

Nearby, the village of Fürstenburg is home to Germany's second-oldest porcelain factory, established in the 18th century. Paderborn is a large, lively university city with a beautifully preserved historic quarter. It has a Weser Renaissance city hall, with a three-gabled façade, and another graceful mansion, the Heisingsche Haus, from the same period. Just north, Detmold was the capital of a small principality until 1918, and its finest monument is still the elegantly turretted princely castle. The old quarter is a delight, particularly the market square.

Brake Castle, in the pretty town of Lemgo, was rebuilt in the Renaissance style in the last years of the 16th century. Surrounded by a moat, and topped with a graceful tower, the complex includes agricultural estate buildings, mills and a wash house. It is now a museum dedicated to the Weser Renaissance, with exhibitions illustrating the period. Lemgo's charming old quarter is a delight to explore on foot, and contains another Renaissance masterpiece: a superb merchant's house dating from 1571, the Hexenbürgermeisterhaus ('House of the Witch Master') has been converted into a fascinating museum.

Neuhaus Castle is the centrepoint of the town of Paderborn. Cultural events are held in the castle's grounds throughout the summer, with outdoor plays, puppet shows and art exhibitions.

The town of Einbeck boasts many fine examples of half-timbered buildings from the Weser Renaissance period, such as this immaculately maintained gable. The term half-timbered refers to a building in which the wooden timbers of the frame are exposed, while the spaces between them are filled with plaster, brick or stone..

Hameln is famous throughout the world thanks to the tale of the Pied Piper who rid the town of its rats with dire consequences. Idyllically set astride the river, with the Weser hills forming an undulating backdrop, it has an immaculate old quarter with half-timbered houses, and a host of Renaissance mansions bearing the ornate façades typical of the Weser style. Among them are the Rattenkrug, constructed in 1568 and the first building to be built in the Weser Renaissance style in the city. While in Hameln, don't miss a stroll down Bungelosenstrasse, the one street in the city where music has been banned in memory of the Pied Piper.

The little spa town of Bad Münder sits serenely on the river bank and has a sprinkling of Renaissance buildings. Upriver, Minden is a pristine medieval town with several remarkable 16th-century buildings, including the gabled city hall, with its unusual arcades. Look out for other townhouses in the Weser Renaissance style, including the Haus Hill and the Haus

Hagemeyer. On the outskirts of town, the Schloss Haddenhausen was built in the early 17th century and is surrounded by idyllic parklands. East of Minden, the town of Bückeburg is dominated by a superb castle, which overhangs the river. Begun in the 14th century, it was substantially remodelled by the Dukes of Schaumberg-Lippe in the early 1600s, and remains the family home. Today the castle, the spectacular family mausoleum, riding school and extensive gardens are open to the public.

Next, the route reaches Nienburg. Curved along the banks of the Weser, the town has an alluring historic kernel with a smattering of half-timbered burgher's houses and arcades, and a splendid city hall with a fine stepped gable. There are stunning views over the old town from the spire of St Martin's Church. Most of the medieval castle was destroyed, but one solid tower survives and has become a landmark. The journey ends in the bustling port city of Bremen.

Today, Bremen is a modern, industrial city, but many fine examples of late medieval architecture are still preserved in the Old Town on the banks of the Weber.

THE GOLDEN CIRCLE

Start Reykjavik **End** Reykjavik	
Countries crossed Iceland	
Distance 300 kilometres (200 miles)	
Transport used Car	
Highlights Reykjavik, Geysir and Strokkur geysers, Gullfoss waterfall, Skálholt church, Thingvellir	

Iceland sits above the Mid-Atlantic Ridge, where the Eurasian and North American plate boundaries meet and jostle. In this apparently frozen land, intense geothermal activity erupts in hot springs, geysers and bubbling mud pools.

The name of the capital city, Reykjavik, means 'Bay of Smoke', possibly a reference to the gusts of steam emitted by the region's hot springs. These remain an intrinsic part of Icelandic life, and the handful of

Reykjavik is the capital of Iceland and the island's oldest settlement, established by Norse settlers in the ninth century AD. The city is full of bustling bars, many of which only really get going after midnight during summer months.

geothermal hot spring complexes scattered around the city are very popular. The heart of the city is the Old Town, Reykjavik's historic core, where several museums tell the story of the island's settlement. Reykjavik has also long been famous for its heady nightlife, especially during the long white nights of summer. From Reykjavik, a day trip makes a scenic loop, known as the Golden Circle, around some of the island.

About 50 kilometres (30 miles) northeast of the capital, the Thingvellir National Park preserves the site of Iceland's first assembly, the Althing, the oldest parliament in Europe, which first gathered here in 930 AD. The rift lake of Thingvallavatn is Iceland's largest freshwater lake, known for the purity of its crystal clear waters. It has become a popular destination for snorkelling and diving. The road skirts the northern end of the lake and enters the strange lunar landscape of the Haukadalur Valley. For all its apparent serenity, this area seethes with subterranean geothermal activity that bubbles up to the surface in the form of hot springs, steam vents and mud pools. This is where Geysir – which has given its name to the phenomenon in English – once jetted high into the air.

The fault line between the North American and Eurasian continental plates, known as the Mid-Atlantic Ridge, cuts through the centre of Iceland. The fault is widening as the continents drift apart at a rate of about 2.5 centimetres (1 in) per year, making the island highly volcanic. Here, bathers enjoy the heat of a geothermal pool.

Before 1916, when Geysir abruptly stopped exploding, it could blast streams of boiling water more than 60 metres (200 ft) high. Now, visitors must be content with nearby Strokkur, which obligingly shoots high columns of steam at roughly ten-minute intervals to the collective gasps of onlookers.

East of the Haukadalur Valley, Iceland's most dramatic waterfall cascades powerfully over shiny black basalt rocks. The force of the water creates a cloud of mist, where rainbows hang on sunny days. Driving south of Gullfoss through the Biskupstungur, stop at the little hamlet of Skálholt. Now little more than a straggle of houses dominated by an immaculate white church, this was once one of the most powerful towns of Iceland, at the heart of the political and religious struggles that dominated its history for several centuries. The current church, consecrated in 1963, is the 11th to occupy this site. An underground vault preserves the sepulchre of Páll Jónsson (1155–1211), a powerful bishop. There is also a museum and a display of illuminated manuscripts. Near Skálholt, a cluster of craters can be found in the Grímsnes region. The largest of these is the Kerid crater, thought to have been created about 3,000 years ago, which contains an emerald green lake.

On the return journey, note the Hellisheidarvirkjun power plant on the right: this harnesses Iceland's natural geothermal energy, producing electricity and directing the hot water to Icelandic homes.

The Skaftafell National Park in Iceland's Sudurland region is known for its agreeable alpine climate and warm days in summer. It is home to several species of birds and arctic foxes. In the Middle Ages, the area was fertile farmland but the farms were abandoned after a series of large volcanic explosions, followed by periods of glaciation.

THE CASTLE ROAD

Start Mannheim **End** Prague

Countries crossed Germany, Czech Republic **Distance** 1,200 kilometres (745 miles)

Transport used Car

Highlights Mannheim, Neckar Valley, Heidelberg, Nuremberg, Bamberg, Bayreuth, Kovel castle, Karlštejn, Prague

The Castle Road (known as the 'Burgenstrasse' in Germany) winds through the hills of southern Germany and into the Czech Republic, twisting past more than 70 castles and palaces, as well as a host of ancient churches, medieval towns and villages. It begins in Mannheim, elegant abode of the Counts Palatine, and culminates in the fairytale city of Prague.

Mannheim sits at the confluence of the Neckar and Rhine rivers. A handsome city of broad avenues and squares, it was laid out in the 17th century by Frederic IV, Count Palatine of the Rhine. A century later, the splendid palace was built, and it is still the largest Baroque castle in Germany. It has since been transformed into the city university.

Sitting between Mannheim and Heidelberg, Schwetzingen Castle dates from the 14th century, but was steadily expanded over succeeding centuries. It served as a summer palace for the Counts Palatine, and is surrounded by magnificent Baroque gardens, filled with fountains and follies.

Farther along the River Neckar is the storybook town of Heidelberg, a huddle of red-tiled roofs crowned by an imposing castle. The Electorate Palatinate resided in Heidelberg for four centuries before moving their court to Mannheim, and the old quarter is full of fine churches and

At one end of the Castle Road, the walls of Hradcany Castle and its cathedral tower over the Czech capital of Prague, while the Charles Bridge spans the Vltava River in the foreground.

mansions, which reflect its early wealth and affluence. The university is one of Europe's oldest and most prestigious, and played an important role in the Reformation.

More winsome villages line the Neckar Valley, still guarded by their medieval castles. At Eberbach, the castle sits amid woodland above the historic town, and handsome little Mosbach is replete with half-timbered houses. The largest and oldest castle in this valley is at Hornberg, and has been converted – like many along this route – into a smart hotel.

The imposing ruins of Heidelberg Castle have a commanding view over the River Neckar. The castle was abandoned in the 18th century and subsequently fell into disrepair.

The parade of castles continues east with the medieval Schloss Neuenstein. It was transformed into a superb Renaissance residence during the 16th century, but has functioned as a museum for the last century and a half. Schwäbisch Hall is perched on a steep crag over the River Kocher. Just east, Rothenburg ob der Tauber is the most perfectly preserved medieval town in Germany, with a fine 12th-century gateway and tranquil gardens. The elaborate Ansbach Castle, rebuilt in flamboyant rococo style during the early 18th century, displays the celebrated local porcelain. Midway along the route lies the city of Nuremberg from where German monarchs ruled the Holy Roman Empire for five centuries. The impressive castle at Nuremberg still dominates the great walled city.

The restored town of Bamberg contains a grand residence, built in the early 17th century for the prince-bishops who ruled the region, and its medieval castle occupies a crag high above the town. Equally picturesque, Coburg preserves a pair of palaces built for the local duchy: the Callenburg Palace was used as a summer retreat for the dukes of Coburg until the 1940s, while the 16th-century Ehrenburg Palace was their main seat. Charming Bayreuth is best known for its association with Richard Wagner, who lived and composed here. The old castle dates back to the 13th century.

Across the border in the Czech Republic is another string of charming spa towns, often topped with elaborate castles. Kynžvart Castle is one of the grandest, rebuilt in the 18th century in the sober Viennese Classicist style. Heading east, the lofty Karlštejn Castle sits on a high crag in order to safeguard the imperial treasures. The journey ends in Prague, 'the Golden City', still guarded by the ethereal walls of a castle on a hill above the Danube.

The fairytale castle of Schloss Sommersdorf was built in the 14th century. Today, it is still a private residence, although some of its rooms are available to travellers as they explore the Castle Road and the nearby Romantic Road (see pages 74–77).

THE DALMATIAN COAST

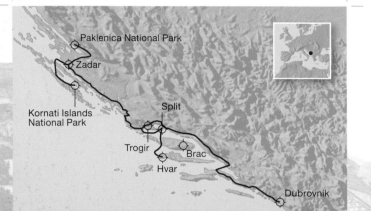

Start Zadar   **End** Dubrovnik

Countries crossed Croatia

Distance 300 kilometres (200 miles)   **Transport used** Ferry and car

Highlights Paklenica National Park, Zadar, Kornati Islands National Park, Trogir, Split, Makarska Riviera, Hvar, Dubrovnik

The Adriatic Sea has sculpted Croatia's Dalmatian Coast into myriad magical bays and inlets, and the azure waters are flecked with more than a thousand islands. The coastline is backed by high mountains, swathed with maquis or forest, and dotted with immaculate medieval towns and ancient ruins. This tour begins in the north, at the walled city of Zadar which occupies a small promontory jutting out into the bay. Zadar is a good base for exploring the Paklenica National Park, a stunning nature reserve set in the Velebit mountains. For snorkelling and diving, head to the island of Dugi Otok, linked to Zadar by ferry.

Biograd, south of Zadar, is the main jumping off point for the Kornati Islands National Park. This stunning archipelago of uninhabited islands is a perfect place to hire a boat and spend a few days exploring. Inland from the peaceful mainland town of Sibenik, the Krka National Park has scores of scenic hiking trails. Trogir, an enchanting medieval harbour town, has a perfectly preserved ensemble of Gothic and Renaissance buildings. Split is Croatia's second-largest city, spread around a huge port. Its kernel is a remarkably well preserved medieval town. Split is also famous for its beaches and nightlife. It's a good base for visiting islands such as Solta and Brac, which are both popular for diving.

The old walls of Dubrovnik were built in the tenth century. The city reached the height of its powers in the 16th century, when it was a centre for maritime trade, and many splendid buildings remain from this time.

The centre of Split is built around the ruins of a vast palace complex. The palace was constructed at the end of the third century AD for the Dalmatian-born Roman Emperor Diocletian, who wanted to return to his homeland for his retirement. After Diocletian's death in 311 AD, the palace fell into ruins, and eventually a town grew up in its midst.

A string of spectacular beaches unfurl south of Split, including those at Onis, Brela Beach and Baska Voda. Makarska is a delightful little port town curled at the foot of the Biokovo mountain, with fine views across to the islands, great beaches, and a network of hiking trails. Drvenik, to the south, is the main port for ferries out to Hvar, one of the most beautiful islands on the coast. Hvar Town was built under the Venetians, and its red-roofed houses are piled up prettily around the port. Korcula Island has a splendid little capital built under the Venetians, as well as dense forests and turquoise bays.

Dubrovnik, the most beguiling city on the Dalmatian Coast, is a citadel of pale stone and red roofs perched at the tip of an isthmus. At its peak, it was the only rival to Venice on the Adriatic, and the plethora of magnificent monuments reflect its history. At the heart of the city is Luža Square, home to a trio of sumptuous buildings: the Baroque church of St Blaise, the handsomely arcaded Rector's Palace, and the Sponza Palace, a Renaissance masterpiece that miraculously survived a massive earthquake in 1667. There are stunning views over the rocky coast from the towers that punctuate the massive walls.

The tranquil port of Milna on the island of Brac. The island is famous for its goat's cheese, wine, olive oil and fine building stone.

THE ITALIAN LAKES

Start Locarno **End** Como

Countries crossed Switzerland, Italy

Distance 240 kilometres (150 miles) **Transport used** Car, ferry

Highlights Locarno, Vabenia, Baverno, Lugano, Villa Favorita (Thyssen-Bornemisza Museum), Gandria, Cadenabbia, Bellagio, Como, historic villas and gardens such as the Villa Carlota

The Italian Lake District, with its Alpine scenery, invigorating air, lavish villas and splendid gardens, has attracted visitors ever since English aristocrats made it an essential stop on the Grand Tour in the early 1800s. By 1906, the Orient Express train company had included Stresa, on the shores of Lake Maggiore, on its luxurious Paris–Venice route. The region still exudes the air of a bygone age, with its grand 19th-century hotels overlooking elegant lakefront promenades, and splendid villas set in luxuriant gardens. This tour takes in the highlights of Lakes Maggiore, Como and Lugano.

The 65-kilometre (40-mile)-long Lake Maggiore is the largest lake in these parts. At its northern end, the Swiss town of Locarno spills down wooded Alpine slopes to the lake. The old quarter boasts cobbled streets, beautiful squares and manicured gardens that line the waterfront. A funicular will take you to the sanctuary of Madonna del Sasso, perched on a cliff high above the town. A panoramic lakeside road links Locarno with the towns to the south. First of these is Ascona, which is set around a fine sheltered harbour. Beyond it to the south is Cannobio, just beyond the Italian border, a huddle of red-roofed houses backed by wooded slopes. Verbania is much larger, and has several splendid 19th-century gardens. The road swings south, over the marshes of the Fondo Toce Nature Reserve, and on to Baveno, where 19th-century visitors from

Lake Como has been a favoured retreat for the wealthy ever since Roman times. Today, it is lined by fine villas and palaces, many belonging to millionaires and film stars.

The idyllic island of Isola Bella sits in the middle of Lake Maggiore, where the Alps tower majestically in the background.

Byron to Queen Victoria came to take the waters (it's still a highly reputed spa town). The surrounding hills are filled with beautiful villas and gardens, including the exotic Villa Barberis, and the 16th-century Villa Brondolini d'Adda. A little farther south of Baveno is the chic little resort of Stresa, which hosts a prestigious classical music festival every summer. Boats depart from the harbour for the Borromean Islands. Isola Maggiore is the largest, with magnificent English-style gardens. On the southern shore of Lake Maggiore is Arona, which has a handsome historic centre dominated by a 17th-century basilica and archbishop's palace.

Head east away from Lake Maggiore and the next lake you come to is Lake Lugano, the smallest of this trio of lakes. The biggest city is Lugano on the northern shore. Walk along the lakefront promenade to Castagnola, where the exquisite 17th-century Villa Favorita now contains the Thyssen-Bornemisza Museum with a superb collection of artworks. To the east, (Swiss) Gandria is beautifully set at the foot of Mont Brè, and offers wonderful mountain scenery. The best views are to be had from the top of Monte Generoso, reached via a funicular railway that trundles through pristine Alpine scenery.

The road continues along the northern shore, reaching Porlezza at the eastern tip. Just a short distance east is Megaggio, which sits on the banks of the Lake Como. Como is perhaps the most beautiful of these three lakes. South of Menaggio, don't miss the opportunity to see the opulent Villa Carlotta in Tremezzo. This 18th-century palace is set amid magnificent gardens arranged in steep terraces above the lake.

Ferries depart from Cadenabbia for Bellagio, often described as the 'Pearl of Lake Como'. This enchanting town is sheltered by a promontory jutting out into the lake, which makes for a remarkable sight when approached by water. Its cobbled streets, large piazzas and romantic waterfront are beautifully preserved. From Bellagio, a minor road follows the lake south to Como, a prosperous and well preserved city enclosed by sweeping mountains, which marks the end of the journey.

TRAVELLER'S TIPS

Best time to go: Visit in spring to see the gardens in full bloom, or early autumn to enjoy the spectacle of the changing leaves. Try to avoid July and August when the roads are impossibly crowded.

Look out for: The region hosts several important music and performing arts festivals from spring until autumn.

Dos and don'ts: Do remember to get a special pass if you are travelling on Swiss motorways.

THE AMALFI COAST

Start Salerno	**End** Sorrento

Countries crossed Italy

Distance 56 kilometres (35 miles)

Transport used Car

Highlights Ravello, Amalfi, Emerald Grotto, Furore fjord, Positano

With its plunging cliffs, sparkling seas, pastel-coloured villages, vineyards and olive groves, it is no surprise that the Amalfi Coast has been inscribed on the UNESCO World Heritage List for its outstanding beauty. A narrow road wriggles along the edge of the region's coastal cliff, linking the glamorous towns and picturesque villages of the Sorrentine peninsula, which is dotted with tranquil coves and historic villas.

Driving north from Salerno, the first stop is Vietri sul Mare, which overlooks a sheltered little bay, and where a Saracen tower still stands. The town has been making its vividly coloured ceramics since the 15th century. Beyond it, little Cetara is still known for anchovy sauce, which varies only slightly from the Roman *garum* made here 2,000 years ago and exported around the empire. To the west, some of the finest beaches on this craggy coast are found at Maiori, one of the most important towns of the Republic of Amalfi, which flourished during the tenth and 11th centuries.

A few kilometres inland from Castiglione, the impregnable mountain town of Ravello was first established as a refuge from the barbarian armies sweeping down the boot of Italy during the sixth century. A graceful town of palaces, churches and gardens, it has long inspired musicians and writers. The 11th-century cathedral is adorned by a slender belltower, which overlooks the Piazza del Vescovado. A plain watchtower on the same square is the unlikely entrance to the lavish Villa Rufolo. The gardens are breathtaking, and offer views out over the hills to the sea. The Villa Cimbrone offers the finest views of all from the celebrated Belvedere of Infinity.

The beautiful Amalfi Coast comprises a rocky coastline punctuated by small, narrow bays. Colourful houses, villages and towns, perched on top of plunging cliffs, face the azure waters of the Tyrrhenian Sea.

The Amalfi region, and in particular Sorrento, is home to countless fragrant lemon groves. The citrus fruit is used to make the digestif liqueur limoncello and the local delicacy delizia al limone.

With its ice-cream coloured houses perched delicately around the bay, Positano embodies the beauty of the Amalfi Coast.

Back along the coast, the ruins of a sumptuous Roman villa can be visited at little Minori, where an open-air theatre is used for outdoor performances in summer. Consider taking a side trip to visit the old-fashioned villages of the Tramonti, where vineyards and orchards spill down the hillside in steep terraces. Little Atrani is full of handsome churches, including the tenth-century Church of San Salvatore de Birecto, where the Dukes of Amalfi were crowned. Neighbouring Amalfi, piled around a sparkling harbour, was once the largest trading port in southern Italy and the capital of a wealthy republic.

Conca dei Marini is an entrancing fishing village built into the cliff above a sheltered bay. There are dizzying views out over the Capo di Vettica promontory at the tip of the Sorrentine peninsula, and the famous Emerald Grotto is filled with remarkable stalagtites and stalagmites, which glint as the deep green water eddies around the cave.

The fishing village of Praiano, piled around a beautiful harbour, is filled with fine churches. It is also the starting point of the Sentiero degli Dei ('Walkway of the Gods'), a magnificent hike through the hills to Agerola. Positano has become a favourite retreat for the fashion crowd, and is packed with stylish hotels and chic boutiques. Although the Amalfi Coast proper ends at Positano, you can extend the drive by continuing to Sorrento, the largest town on the peninsula. This seaside resort is magnificently set on the Bay of Naples, with fine views along the coast and up to Mount Vesuvius. Sorrento is also the convenient starting point for ferries to the captivating islands of Capri and Ischia.

TRAVELLER'S **TIPS**

Best time to go: This drive is best in June or late September, when the roads are less crowded. Avoid August.

Look out for: The road is the main bus route from Sorrento to Salerno, which can make the narrow road even more hair-raising than usual.

Dos and don'ts: Do try the local specialities, particularly the distinctive lemon liqueur limoncello.

THE SILK ROUTE

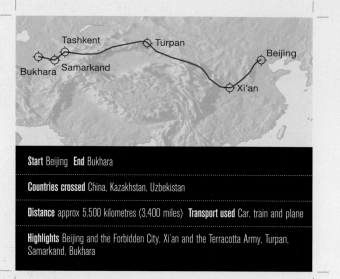

Start Beijing **End** Bukhara

Countries crossed China, Kazakhstan, Uzbekistan

Distance approx 5,500 kilometres (3,400 miles) **Transport used** Car, train and plane

Highlights Beijing and the Forbidden City, Xi'an and the Terracotta Army, Turpan, Samarkand, Bukhara

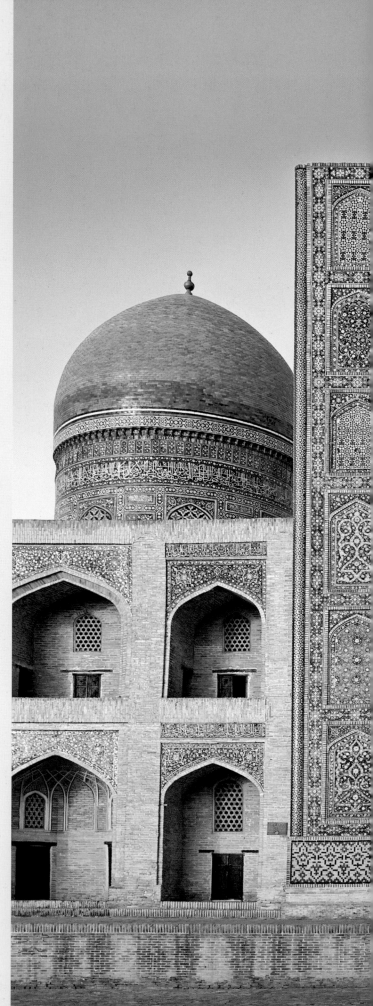

The Silk Road is a network of trade routes that connected East and West by land and sea, and which gained its name from the most precious commodity traded along its length. The routes were established more than 2,000 years ago and reached their peak in the second century AD.

Beijing has been China's capital for more than a thousand years. At the heart of the soaring, neon-lit city is the Forbidden Palace, a dazzling complex of palaces, squares and temples hidden behind huge walls. Built in the 15th century, it was home to the imperial family and court until 1912, when the last Chinese emperor was forced to abdicate. The Temple of Heaven, in the south of the city, is magnificently decorated and carefully laid out to reflect the relationship between heaven and earth in Chinese cosmogony. This is where successive emperors prayed for a good harvest.

To the southwest lies Xi'an, the eastern terminus of this ancient trading route. Also known as 'the eternal city', Xi'an preceded Beijing as capital and was the seat of the imperial court. It preserves a wealth of extraordinary monuments, including the huge city walls, ancient mausolea and spectacular temples. According to legend, 700,000 labourers were needed to build the mausoleum of Emperor Qin Shi Huang (259–210 BC), which is guarded by thousands of life-sized warriors – the Terracotta Army.

The Uygar city of Turpan, surrounded by harsh desert in northeast China, has provided weary travellers with respite for centuries. It sits 154 metres (505 ft) below sea level in the Turpan Depression, the lowest place on Earth after the Dead Sea, but thanks to the ingenious 'karez' well system, in use for millennia,

Built opposite the Kalyan Mosque in Bukhara in the 1530s, the ornate Mir-i Arab Madrasa is still in use as a centre for Islamic education.

The tomb of Emperor Qin Shi Huang is guarded by the Terracotta Army, made up of thousands of individually carved, life-sized soldiers and horses that were placed in the tomb to fight for Huang's empire in the afterlife.

Turpan's fertile fields produce excellent fruit, particularly grapes. To the south of the city, the ruins of Gaochang, a garrison town on the Silk Road, have been bleached white by the searing sun, and, to the east, in the Flaming Mountains, Buddhist caves have been discovered hollowed into the rocks.

Kashgar, at the border with Kyrgyzstan, is located at the crux of major trading routes on the Silk Road. It has a rambling historic core and a smattering of fine monuments including a 15th-century mosque.

Tashkent is the modern, largely Soviet-built capital of Uzbekistan. Once one of the most beautiful cities in Asia, it was badly damaged during the Russian Revolution in 1917 and destroyed by an earthquake in 1966. Hints of its former magnificence survive in the chaotic Old Town, where, under the modern dome of the Chorsu Bazaar, every imaginable object is bought and sold in an atmosphere that has changed little since the old days of the Silk Road. Some exquisitely tiled

religious buildings, including the 16th-century madrasas (Islamic academies) of Kukeldash and Barak Khan, survived the earthquake.

As old as Rome or Babylon, the ancient city of Samarkand stands on an ancient crossroads. Conquered by Alexander the Great in 329 BC and reduced to rubble by Genghis Khan, Samarkand flowered during the 14th century under Timur, who made it the capital of his empire and the greatest city of Central Asia. At its heart is the Registan, a majestic square lined since Timur's time with madrasas. Turquoise-tiled domes, delicate minarets and intricate mosaics shimmer under the burning sun. In the shadow of the Bibi-Khanym Mosque, trading continues much as it has for centuries in the chaotic bazaar. The Shah-i Zinde mausoleum contains the tomb of the Muslim martyr Qutham ibn Abbas, slain while protecting the city in the eighth century, while Timur is buried beneath a huge jade slab close to the Registan.

The holy city of Bukhara is a sun-baked ochre settlement which has long been stripped of the opulent tiles and gilding that still dazzle in Samarkand. But Bukhara can claim a history at least as long as its rival's. Established, according to legend, a thousand years before the arrival of Alexander the Great, it became a centre of learning renowned throughout the Islamic world. Even now, it contains more than 350 mosques, of which the most beautiful is the Magoki-Attori mosque, and a hundred madrasas. Another major commercial hub of the Silk Road, three of five 16th-century trading domes still survive. Above them towers the 12th-century Kaliyan Minaret, once the tallest building in Asia and a watchtower and lighthouse for trade caravans.

A few hours travel from Kashgar lies the beautiful lake of Karakul. Located high on the Pamir Plateau, travellers are drawn here by the lake's pristine waters and the staggering views of its surrounding peaks, including the Kunlun and Tien Shan mountain ranges.

TRAVELLER'S TIPS

Best time to go: Spring and autumn are the best times to visit, in order to avoid the searing summer temperatures and the winter cold.

Look out for: Given the unsettled political climate of central Asia, it is recommended that visitors use a reputable tour company for travelling the Silk Road. Independent travel is particularly difficult in Uzbekistan.

Dos and don'ts: Do ensure that you have all the relevant visas and entry permits before travel. Do be sensitive to local cultures and dress accordingly.

123

THE TRANS-SIBERIAN EXPRESS

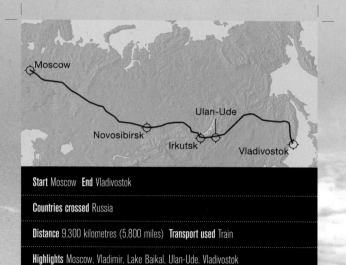

Start Moscow **End** Vladivostok

Countries crossed Russia

Distance 9,300 kilometres (5,800 miles) **Transport used** Train

Highlights Moscow, Vladimir, Lake Baikal, Ulan-Ude, Vladivostok

The Trans-Siberian Railway in Russia was built between 1891 and 1916 to link Moscow with Vladivostok, nearly 10,000 kilometres (6,000 miles) away on the Pacific Coast. The train takes seven days to complete the journey, crossing two continents and seven time zones. It chugs past the Ural Mountains, under the endless skies of the vast Siberian steppes and past the world's oldest and deepest lake, Baikal. Although it is now popular with tourists, the route also remains an important transport link for domestic travellers and freight.

Moscow is one of the world's greatest cities, a vast metropolis straddling the Moskva River. The fortified citadel of the Kremlin, once the imperial residence, is a city-within-a-city, comprising several palaces and cathedrals. It flanks Red Square, which is ringed with impressive monuments including the lavishly decorated cathedral of St Basil. The colourfully tiled onion domes of this 16th-century church have become a much-loved symbol of the city. The turn-of-the-20th-century Yaroslavl Rail Terminal, with its fairytale spires and towers, is a fittingly picturesque starting point for the great Trans-Siberian railway.

From Moscow the train begins its journey east, reaching Vladimir after 200 kilometres (120 miles). Vladimir is a small, historic city scattered with reminders of its glorious heyday as the capital of a small kingdom. Finest of these are the 12th-century Golden Gates at the entrance to the city and the Assumption Cathedral from the same period. Another day's travelling brings you to the Ural Mountains, the historic geographical divider between the continents of Europe and Asia. The unofficial capital of the Urals is Ekaterinaburg,

Lake Baikal is home to a huge variety of flora and fauna found nowhere else in the world, including the Baikal seal. Over 30 million years old and with an average depth of 750 metres (2,500 ft), the lake is the oldest and deepest lake on Earth.

Herders shepherd their caribou through the harsh Siberian landscape. Between October and March the temperature rarely rises above freezing, although the short Siberian summer can be surprisingly warm.

125

The multicoloured onion domes of St Basil's Cathedral in Red Square, Moscow, mark the centre of the great city.

founded in the 18th century, and now a large and dynamic industrial city. It was here that the last Tsar of Russia, Nicholas II, was executed in 1918.

The vast steppe unfolds east of the Urals, the meadows scattered with bright wildflowers in spring. Here the railway passes through Novosibirsk on the Ob River, 3,300 kilometres (2,000 miles) from Moscow. It is the third-largest city in Russia after Moscow and St Petersburg. Its name means 'New Siberian City', and it was founded in 1893 as the site of a bridge over the Ob for the Trans-Siberian Railway. The bridge was opened in 1897, at which time Novosibirsk was a small town of 7,800 people. Today it is a busy metropolis with nearly 1.5 million inhabitants.

Irkutsk, at 5,150 kilometres (3,200 miles) from Moscow, is roughly half way along the route, and is reached on the third day. The city is the most popular stopover for travellers on the Trans Siberian Railway, thanks to its location at the southern end of the enormous Lake Baikal. This lake is the world's oldest and deepest, and so incredibly biodiverse that it has been called 'the Galápagos of Russia'. Surrounded by mountains and forests, its blue waters reflect the shifting skies overhead. The train line skirts the magnificent lake and heads to Ulan-Ude, capital of the Buryati Republic. Now a tranquil little city, it still retains several traditional wooden Buryat buildings, which contrast with the Soviet-era architecture.

Next the route takes you to remote Birodzhan, 8,300 kilometres (5,150 miles) and five days from Moscow. Established by Stalin as a centre for Jewish settlement, Birodzhan still boasts two impressive synagogues. Here, the train crosses the Amur River. The railway skirts the Chinese border before arriving finally at the huge seaport of Vladivostok on the Pacific Ocean. It's a scruffy, atmospheric city, with mouldering 19th-century warehouses and buildings in the centre, set around a wide bay enclosed by steep hills.

TRAVELLER'S TIPS

Best time to go: May to September, with July and August being the busiest months.

Look out for: The luxury Golden Eagle tourist train also makes the journey, and in considerably more comfort.

Dos and don'ts: Do book well ahead for tickets, particularly in July and August. Do research your journey carefully: trains vary widely in terms of comfort and not all make stops.

THE GANGES

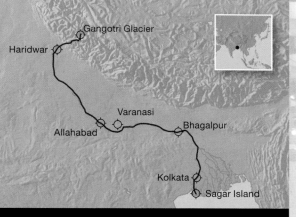

Start Gangotri Glacier **End** Sagar Island
Countries crossed India
Distance 2,500 kilometres (1,500 miles) **Transport used** Car
Highlights Gangotri Glacier, Haridwar, Allahabad, Varanasi, Bhagalpur, Kolkata, Sagar Island

The Ganges, India's greatest river, flows for more than 2,500 kilometres (1,500 miles) from its source in the Himalayas, across a densely populated plain and into the Bay of Bengal. The river is the lifeline of India and millions depend on the waters for drinking, washing, irrigation and industry. Above all, however, it is revered as the embodiment of the goddess Ganga. This sacred river is said to cure illnesses, offer absolution from sins, and dying on its banks ensures a direct route to heaven.

The river emerges from an ice cave beneath the Gangotri Glacier. Pilgrims inhabit caves and huts around the sacred source, and Devprayag, the first sizeable settlement along the Ganges, is full of Hindu priests and holy men. The road carves through the Himalayan foothills before reaching the sacred town of Rishikesh, full of temples and shrines. Just south of Rishikesh, the river reaches the north Indian plains at Haridwar, one of the seven holiest cities in the Hindu religion. Legend relates that it was one of the four sites where the celestial bird Garuda let fall some drops of *amrit*, the elixir of immortality. The spot is now the most important shrine in the city.

Pilgrims pray at Haridwar during the Kumbha Mela, a mass pilgrimage to the Ganges that takes place every three years. Washing in the sacred waters is said to cleanse both the spirit and the body.

Religious offerings and oil lamps float on the currents of the Ganges near the ancient holy city of Varanasi, also known as Benares, in the state of Uttar Pradesh. Varanasi is one of the oldest continually inhabited cities in the world, dating from the third millennium BC, near the very beginning of civilization.

Best time to go: Most of the largest religious celebrations take place in winter (November to February). Avoid travelling during the summer, if possible, to avoid the heat and monsoons.

Look out for: Most of the cities, particularly Varanasi and Allahabad, offer boat rides on the river.

Dos and don'ts: Parts of this region can be politically volatile, so check in advance whether it is safe to travel or not.

The festival of Kumbha Mela celebrates this event every three years in each of the four sacred cities, and attracts millions of Hindu pilgrims. The Har-ki Pauri, an elaborate staircase (ghat) leading down to the river, is said to stand where the river leaves the Himalayas for the plains, and is adorned with a large footprint, believed to be that of Lord Vishnu himself. Each night, people gather here to sing the praises of Ganga, as priests chant and float candles along the river.

The Kumbha Mela is also celebrated at Allahabad, another 700 kilometres (450 miles) to the east, which sits at the confluence of three holy rivers and has even deeper religious significance. Pilgrims come to bathe in the Triveni Sangam, the holy meeting point of the waters. The second oldest city in India, Hindus believe that it was here at Allahabad that Brahma, who created the universe, made his first sacrifice.

Varanasi, also called Benares and Kashi, or 'City of Light', is the holiest city in the Hindu world, piled steeply above the banks of the Ganges. Here, multitudes of pilgrims gather daily at the ghats to wash themselves in the sacred waters.

Some 500 kilometres (300 miles) east, the great river flows through fertile plains and passes the ancient silk-making city of Bhagalpur. The city appears in a number of ancient Indian epics, and Hindus believe that Mandar Hill, 50 kilometres (30 miles) to the south, was used to churn the ocean in order to produce *amrit*, the elixir of immortality. The hill is said to have kept the imprint of the snake god, Vasuki, and Bhagalpur celebrates the festival of Vish-hari Puja in honour of Manasa Devi, the daughter of Lord Shiva and the Queen of Snakes.

At Kolkata, the Ganges fans out to create a vast delta on its way to the sea. Kolkata sits on the Hooghly River, one of the largest tributaries, and is a comparatively new city by Indian standards – it was founded by the British in 1698.

The river finally disgorges into the sea in the Bay of Bengal. At the western end of the Ganges Delta, Sagar Island is revered as the departure point of the Mother River and is scattered with shrines and temples. The southern tip of the island is the focal point of a huge annual festival, when hundreds of thousands of pilgrims descend on the island to bathe in the holy waters.

Kolkata is filled with reminders of India's colonial past. The city was once the capital of the British Raj and its monuments include the Victoria Memorial, a building dedicated to the Empress of India, Queen Victoria, in 1921.

THE GRAND TRUNK ROAD

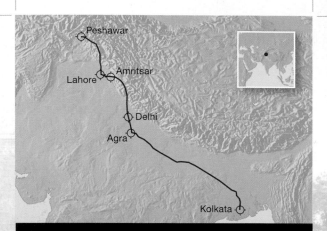

Start Peshawar, Pakistan **End** Kolkata, India

Countries crossed Pakistan and India

Distance 2,500 kilometres (1,550 miles) **Transport used** Car

Highlights Peshawar, Attock, Islamabad, Rawalpindi, Taxila, Lahore, Amritsar, Delhi, Agra, Varanasi, Kolkata

The Grand Trunk Road sweeps from Pakistan, across northern India to the border with Bangladesh, following a natural corridor along which goods, religions and armies have travelled for centuries. It connects many of India's most beautiful and historic cities, including Delhi, Agra and Varanasi, before culminating in Kolkata. For all the modern trappings acquired over recent decades, its spirit has changed little since Rudyard Kipling described it as 'the road of Hindustan' which bore 'such a river of life as nowhere else exists in the world'.

The western terminus is Peshawar, in Pakistan, which sits near the Khyber Pass, on the border with Afghanistan. In the Old City, the teeming streets are filled with auto-rickshaws (tuk tuks) and crowds of a dozen different ethnicities, and the bazaars are piled high with produce, textiles and handicrafts. The sturdy Bela Hisar Fort still guards the city, as it has for almost two centuries.

To the southeast, the road leads to Attock, a historic frontier town on the banks of the great River Indus which is dominated by a mighty Mughal fortress. Farther west are the twin cites of Islamabad, the capital of Pakistan, and Rawalpindi, a former British garrison town. Although it stands at the crossroads of ancient trading routes, Islamabad was only built in the 1960s and is a blur of concrete and steel. Rawalpindi is now a rapidly

The Taj Mahal shimmers in the dawn light. The building is decorated in highly ornate carvings as well as various passages from the Qur'an.

TRAVELLER'S **TIPS**

Best time to go: Avoid the stifling summer heat and visit between October and March.

Look out for: Expect the border crossings to take anything from 30 minutes to 3 hours.

Dos and don'ts: Do arrange visas in advance. Do find out about local festivals and pilgrimages before travelling.

If you're travelling through India in February and March don't miss the spectacular festival of Holi, which marks the beginning of spring. The main day is celebrated by throwing brightly coloured powder and water over everybody in a riot of fun. In the evening, bonfires are lit.

expanding modern city, but its colourful bazaars and battered colonial architecture lend it a raffish charm. About 30 kilometres (19 miles) north of the city, are the remnants of the ancient city of Taxila, which dates back to the sixth century BC.

East of Rawalpindi, the imposing citadel of Rawat Fort, built by the Gakhars in the 16th century, offers spectacular views over the landscape. Lahore shimmers in the distance, the cultural heart of Pakistan for more than a thousand years. At its heart is the Inner City, a tightly packed maze enclosed by a ring of medieval walls. This is overlooked by Lahore Fort, a sumptuously decorated citadel built for the Mughal emperors,

who ruled a vast area that covered most of what is now Pakistan and India between the 16th and 19th centuries.

The road crosses into India at Wagah, where jostling crowds stream across the border. The city of Amritsar is 30 kilometres (19 miles) from the border and it is famous for the Golden Temple. The road continues east along the flat Punjabi plain, carrying bullock carts and bicycles, before it approaches the teeming metropolis of Delhi. This is one of the largest and oldest cities in the world, and has been continuously inhabited for more than 2,500 years. The battered centre of Old Delhi is filled with ancient monuments squeezed around the majestic Red Fort, an Imperial residence built under the Mughals. India's largest mosque, the lavishly decorated Jama Masjid, was built for Shah Jahan, and completed in 1648.

In Agra, the Taj Mahal, the world's greatest monument to love, was built by Shah Jahan for his third and best-loved wife,

Mumtaz Mahal. The finest craftsmen of the age were summoned, and the great domed mausoleum is decorated with marble, precious jewels and stuccowork.

Traversing the densely populated Gangetic plain, the next stop is the sacred city of Varanasi, where elaborate *ghats* ('staircases') line the banks of the Ganges River. For Hindus, the Ganges is the most sacred of their seven sacred rivers, and Varanasi is the *tirtha*, or 'crossing place', where the mortal and divine worlds meet. The city is also sacred to Buddhists, who believe that Buddha gave his first sermons here.

From Varanasi, the countryside becomes greener as it enters the wetlands of the Ganges Delta. The Grand Trunk Road ends at Kolkata. Chaotic and overcrowded, the city is still strewn with colonial monuments such as Fort William and stately mansions filled with rare artworks.

Pigeons fly over the Wazir Khan Mosque in the walled city of Old Lahore, Pakistan. The mosque was completed in 1635 during the reign of Mughal Emperor Shah Jahan. The red brick walls that once surrounded and fortified the old city were destroyed shortly after the British annexed the Punjab in 1849 and were replaced with gardens, but a few of the ancient gates still stand.

THE KII PENINSULA

Start Koyasan **End** Yoshingo

Countries crossed Japan

Distance 560 kilometres (350 miles)

Transport used Car

Highlights Mount Koya, Ryujin Onsen, Kumano shrines, Yoshino

The Kii mountains in central Japan have been sacred to the Japanese for thousands of years. Pilgrimage routes link the holy mountains of Yoshino and Omine, Kumano Sanzan and Koyasan, with the historic capitals of Nara and Kyoto. While these routes retain their deep spiritual significance to the Japanese, who undergo pilgrimages dressed in white pilgrim's robes, they are also increasingly popular hiking areas.

From Osaka, drive south east to the base of Mount Koya (Koyasan), then take the cable car to the summit, where there is a vast temple complex. Called the Kongobu-ji, it contains more than 100 temples and shrines, and has developed into a small town over the centuries. This is one of the country's most important pilgrimage sites and the centre of Shingon ('Pure Word') Buddhism in Japan. About half of the temples function as *shukubu*, hostels where visitors may stay overnight. The much-revered founder of the Shingon sect in Japan, Kobo Daishin, is buried here in the Okunoin temple.

This region is blessed with countless *onsen* (natural hot springs), where walkers and pilgrims can soak tired bones under the stars. A drive south will bring you to Ryujin Onsen, where an inn has been accepting guests since 1657. The following day, drive southeast to find the town of Hongu, which is a good base for exploring the superb Kumano shrines. This trio of Shinto shrines are gathered deep in primeval forest in the southeastern corner of the Kii mountains.

Drive north to Kumano along the coast, then strike inland along twisting mountain roads to reach Yoshino. This sleepy mountain town is trimmed with traditional wooden houses and tea-rooms, where you can sit out on a bamboo balcony, a bowl of green tea in hand, and listen to the sound of conch shells being blown by mountain priests across the forested peaks. Pilgrims pray here before starting off on their 80-km (50-mile) journey to Mount Omine, passing through dense forest scattered with innumerable springs and waterfalls.

Cherry trees in full blossom on the slopes of Mount Yoshimo. During the cherry blossom season, many Japanese families come to picnic under the trees. They follow blossom forecasts in the media that tell them which day to turn up.

Seiganto-ji Temple is one of the three Kumano temples in the Kii mountains. It was built overlooking the Nachi Falls and is believed to be inhabited by a *kami* (spirit) called Hiryu Gogen.

THE GARDEN ROUTE

| **Start** Heidelberg **End** Storm's River **Countries crossed** South Africa |
| **Distance** 300 kilometres (200 miles) **Transport used:** Car |
| **Highlights** Heidelberg, Mossel Bay, George, Garden Route National Park, Plettenberg, wildlife, hiking, whale-watching |

The Garden Route is a stretch of dramatic coastline that encompasses everything from remote headlands to charming resorts, and from pristine lakes to primeval forest. Much of its magnificent natural beauty is preserved in the enormous Garden Route National Park, which provides opportunities for everything from hiking and kayaking to birdwatching and fishing. One of the most popular activities along this coast is whale-watching: almost 40 species of whale and dolphin are found in these waters.

Heidelberg, 'the gateway to the Garden Route', is a tranquil town, which sits amid lush fields on the banks of the Duivenhoks River. It preserves a clutch of historic buildings but is best known as a destination for birdwatchers and walkers. From here, head east to Mossel Bay, the place where Portuguese explorer Bartolomeu Dias first set foot on South African soil when he rounded the Cape of Good Hope in 1488. Now the town has developed into one of the largest and most popular beach resorts in the region, famous for its endless golden sands washed by the warm waters of the Indian Ocean. The distant Outeniqua Mountains shelter the town and ensure it enjoys a balmy climate year-round. Farther along the coast, Herolds Bay, a small hamlet curled around a rocky bay, has retained its old-fashioned, village atmosphere. A favourite with families, the little resort has a sandy beach sheltered by forested headlands.

The mouth of the Keurbooms River meets the Garden Route in Western Cape Province. The Garden Route is a popular and scenic stretch of the southeastern coast of South Africa. It stretches from Mossel Bay in the Western Cape to the Storm's River in neighbouring Eastern Cape.

The next destination along the route is George, another lively resort. It is one of the oldest towns in South Africa, and contains several historic sights, including the 'Slave Tree', an ancient oak with a lock embedded in its trunk. (The lock actually came from a long defunct lawnmower, but local legend attributes it to slaves.) The city was founded on timber, and furniture-making remains an important craft in the region. About 15 kilometres (10 miles) inland from George, the Montagu Pass slices through the Outeniqua Mountains, providing an exhilarating drive with spectacular views.

Stretching east of George is a wild, unspoilt landscape of cliffs, forests, rivers and lagoons. This area is preserved in the vast Garden Route National Park. The Wilderness section of the park is the closest to George, a bucolic landscape of limpid lakes and rivers set against forested hills and mountains. There are wonderful hiking and biking trails, or you can rent a kayak to explore the quiet estuaries and perhaps catch a glimpse of

the extraordinary bird life (which includes various species of kingfisher, heron and egret, as well as the elusive Knysna loerie, famous for its brilliant plumage). The village of Wilderness is the best base for exploring the eastern portion of the park.

Next to Wilderness is the Knysna Lake Area, where numerous lakes and lagoons indent the coastline, backed by dense forest. There are several boardwalks and trails through the nature reserve, which is home to the only forest elephants in South Africa. Very few (the current estimate is just three) of these magnificent animals survive in the wild, but you can visit elephants at the Knysna Elephant Park.

Next along the coast is Plettenberg Bay, piled steeply above the shores at the cusp of South Africa's Eastern and Western Capes. One of the oldest settlements along this coast, it has a smattering of historic buildings including the 18th-century

The Garden Route is known for the diversity of flora thriving in the mild climate of the Cape. The African lily, native to the Cape of Good Hope, adds lavish colour to the coastline.

Old Rectory, built by the Dutch East India Trading Company. Plettenburg Bay is now a buzzing resort, famous for its long beaches, giddy nightlife and an array of activities – everything from sailing to water-skiing is available here. The long sandy beaches are a big draw, but it is possible to find respite from the crowds in the surrounding rivers and estuaries, which can be explored on foot or by canoe.

The magnificent Tsitsikamma Forest, which comprises the western section of the Garden Route National Park, gets its name from a Khoisan word meaning 'place of much water' and encompasses wild, wave-whipped coastline, rivers, gorges and estuaries. This is the largest swathe of indigenous forest in South Africa. There are several superb hiking trails through the park, as well as activities such as the thrilling canopy tours, which allow visitors to explore the forest from above. The main base for these activities is Storm's River, which also marks the official end of the Garden Route.

Mossel Bay lies east of the Cape of Good Hope and west of Knysna on the Garden Route. The warm waters of the Indian Ocean and the protective barrier of the Outeniqua Mountains to the north combine to create idyllic year-round weather patterns, so that the town is reputed to have the finest weather in South Africa.

THE AFRICAN LAKES

Start Victoria Falls **End** Zanzibar	
Countries crossed Tanzania, Zambia, Malawi, Zimbabwe	
Distance 2,000 kilometres (1,200 miles)	
Transport used 4x4	
Highlights Victoria Falls, Hwange National Park, Lake Malawi, Mikumi National Park, Dar es Salaam, Zanzibar	

This overland journey through central and eastern Africa begins at one of the seven great natural wonders of the world: Victoria Falls, the largest waterfall on Earth. The falls mark the frontier between Zimbabwe and Zambia, and each side of the falls offers a different perspective and a range of activities. Victoria Falls is the main town on the Zimbabwean side, while Livingstone, named after the first European explorer to see the falls, is the biggest local hub in Zambia. A number of adrenalin-charged activities can be arranged in both towns, including bungee-jumping, helicopter rides and whitewater rafting. There are national parks on either side of the falls, each with a network of walking trails and viewing points. These offer spectacular views, but also allow for glimpses of elephant, giraffe, zebra and hippopotamus. About an hour's drive south of Victoria Falls, the Hwange National Park is the largest game reserve in Zimbabwe, with more bird and animal species than anywhere else in the country.

Crossing into Zambia, through Livingstone, the journey continues upriver to Lake Kariba. This is the world's largest artificial lake, vast and serene, and it is scattered with islands and surrounded by lush vegetation, game reserves and a smattering of local villages. It is more than 220 kilometres (125 miles) long and up to 40 kilometres (25 miles) wide, and would take days to explore thoroughly, but you can get a taste of its myriad attractions by taking a cruise on one of the house boats that regularly ply the lake's waters. A canoe trip can offer a more intimate experience, as well as fishing opportunities (a very popular activity in the lake's teeming waters). There is even the chance of being rewarded with the astounding sight of elephants bathing in the lake's shallows.

Locally, Victoria Falls is known as *Mosi-o-Tunya*, which means 'the Smoke that Thunders', because the waters cascade with such force into the canyon below that they throw up huge clouds of mist filled with rainbows.

A herd of African elephants makes its way towards a waterhole in the Hwange National Park, in Matabeleland, Zimbabwe.

A jeep ride through southern Zambia leads to Lusaka, the capital, a modern city that sits on a high plateau. Its lively markets are one of the city's biggest draws – the colourful stalls are heaped high with everything from fruit to car tyres.

Lake Malawi lies two days' drive away, across the Malawi border and past the Malawian capital of Lilongwe. Also called Lake Nyasa, it is the third largest and second deepest lake in Africa, and its placid waters are filled with more species of fish than anywhere else on earth. The crystal clear lake is perfect for swimming and snorkelling, as well as more active sports such as windsurfing and sailing. There are several local villages, where visitors can haggle for bargains at the markets, or perhaps try out the dugout canoes which locals use for fishing.

On the other side of the Tanzanian border, the road climbs through the luxuriant tea and banana plantations that extend across the southern Tanzanian highlands. The road scythes through the Mikumi National Park, a spectacular nature reserve replete with wildlife, which adjoins the Selous, Africa's largest reserve. At the centre of the Mikumi is the Mkata floodplain, home to lion, elephant, zebra, wildebeest, giraffe and eland, as well as more than 400 species of bird.

Dar es Salaam is the largest city in Tanzania, a sprawling modern conurbation spread around a natural harbour on the Indian Ocean. Although it offers little to visitors, interesting excursions can be made to surrounding attractions, such as the ancient city of Bagamoyo, formerly an important slave trading town, and the Dar es Salaam Marine Reserve, which comprises four uninhabited islands surrounded by coral reefs.

But the jewel in Tanzania's crown is undoubtedly the Zanzibar archipelago, reached by ferry from Dar es Salaam. The main island sits 25 kilometres (16 miles) from the mainland, surrounded by the calm turquoise waters of the Indian Ocean. It has long been famous for its spices, and the beaches, long stretches of white sand fringed with palm trees, are paradisiacal. The island is ringed with coral reefs, where brilliantly hued fish dart through translucent waters. At the heart of Zanzibar City is Stone Town, which has been an important East African trading settlement for centuries, and is filled with romantically crumbling 18th- and 19th-century buildings.

TRAVELLER'S TIPS

Best time to go: This tour can be done year-round, but travel between August and October for the best chance of seeing wildlife, or in May and June to see the Victoria Falls at their most powerful.

Look out for: Local villages often allow visitors to see the schools and other community buildings.

Dos and don'ts: Do ensure that you are up to date with vaccinations and inoculations before travel.

MOUNT KILIMANJARO

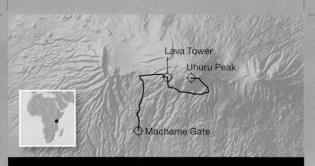

Start Mt Kilimanjaro **End** Mt Kilimanjaro

Countries crossed Tanzania

Distance 40–90 kilometres (25–55 miles) **Transport used** On foot

Highlights Gilman's Point, Uhuru Peak, Lava Tower, glaciers on summit

Mount Kilimanjaro sits just north of the equator. At its base, wildebeest graze on the blazing hot grasslands. Climbers pass through a wide range of habitats on their way to the snow-capped peak.

Mount Kilimanjaro (5,895 metres/19,341 ft) is the highest mountain in Africa. It is also the tallest freestanding mountain in the world. There are several routes up 'Kili', as the mountain is affectionately known, and none requires mountaineering expertise.

The most popular route is the Marangu Route which, at five to six days, is also the shortest. It is the trail that most closely follows the route taken by Hans Meyer (the first European explorer to reach the summit) in 1889. It is often mistakenly perceived as the easiest ascent, but in fact a smaller percentage of climbers reach the summit on the Marangu Route than on any other.

The Machame Route takes six to seven days. It is one of the most scenic routes, taking in cloud forest in Kilimanjaro's lower slopes, and passing groves of the strange senecio plants endemic to East Africa. The Rongai Route (six to seven days) is the only one which begins on the north of the mountain, near the border with Kenya. It is one of the most demanding trails.

The Umbwe Route (six to seven days) is the most difficult of all, a steep ascent that is only suitable for extremely fit climbers. Like Rongai, it is comparatively quiet, making it more likely that you will glimpse wildlife. The Lemosho Route is one of the longest and most beautiful routes up Mount Kilimanjaro, but is rarely used.

At around 4,000 metres (13,000 ft), the routes meet at the Kibo Circuit, a path that loops around the Kibo summit, the biggest of the three craters on the mountain. At the southern end of the crater is Uhuru Peak – the highest point in Africa and the goal of every climber.

TRAVELLER'S **TIPS**

Best time to go: The peak season for climbing Kilimanjaro is July and August: the shoulder seasons are a little less busy. Don't attempt the climb in the rainy season.

Look out for: Kilimanjaro cannot be climbed independently, so you will need to use a reputable tour company.

Dos and don'ts: Do remember to tip guides and porters at the end of the climb.

147

SAILING DOWN THE NILE

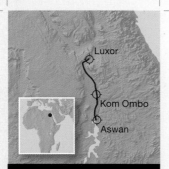

Start Aswan **End** Luxor

Countries crossed Egypt

Distance 200 kilometres (125 miles)

Transport used Felucca (boat)

Highlights Aswan, Elephantine, traditional life on the Nile, Kom Ombo, Luxor

Egypt is a desert country, parched and arid but for the long fertile strip that flanks the Nile, the world's longest river. It flows for 6,650 kilometres (4,130 miles) on its journey from the central African plains to the Mediterranean Sea. The Nile has been the lifeline of Egypt for thousands of years, and more than 90 per cent of the Egyptian population live on or near its banks. Until the construction of the Aswan Dam, the annual flooding of the Nile was crucial to Egypt's very existence.

A traditional Egyptian felucca is carried down the Nile. The rocky desert beyond the river's western bank, seen here below the moon, was believed to mark the entrance to the underworld, and Egypt's royal tombs are located there.

Feluccas – traditional, single-masted boats with white sails – still ply the Nile, just as they have for millennia. Often dwarfed by modern cruiseships, they offer a time-honoured alternative to the tourist motorboats and liners linking the ancient cities of Aswan and Luxor.

Modern Aswan was ancient Swenet, a frontier town and trading settlement established on the border with Nubia. Trade remains a way of life, particularly in the bustling markets and bazaars, and along the busy waterfront. The Nile is shallow here, its waters divided by rocky outcrops and islands, the most important of which is Elephantine. This island preserves a Nilometer, an ancient device used to measure the all-important annual flood, and a vast temple dedicated to Khnum, the god of the Nile who controlled its waters.

A graceful cruise down the river on board a felucca reveals scenes of traditional life along the Nile's shores: fishermen in small wooden boats toss their nets to catch fish, while farmers plough their fields with oxen. The banks of the river are intensely cultivated and surprisingly verdant, providing a startling contrast with the sun-bleached stone of the villages and dwellings dotted among them.

The huge temple Kom Ombo is an impressive sight, towering over the Nile about 45 kilometres (28 miles) downriver from Aswan. Built in the second century BC, the temple is, unusually, dedicated to two gods: Sobek, the crocodile-headed god of fertility, and Horoeris, a form of the falcon-headed god Horus, famed for his healing powers. Sacred crocodiles were raised in the temple's precincts, and mummified after death.

You can still see some of these mummies in a small chapel. These waters were once infested with crocodiles and it was believed that worshipping them would keep the locals safe.

The culmination of the journey is Luxor, ancient Thebes, the glittering capital of Egypt for millennia. The city reached the peak of its glory during the 18th dynasty (c.1550–1292 BC), when the beauty of its temples, palaces and tombs was unsurpassed. Temples are clustered on the east bank of the river, including the staggering Temple of Karnak, the largest religious site anywhere in the world. The west bank is occupied by mausolea and mortuary chapels, including the celebrated Valley of the Kings, which contains more than 60 tombs, including that of young King Tutankhamun.

A stylized representation of Queen Nefertari being led by the hand of the goddess Isis adorns the wall of the queen's tomb in the Valley of the Queens, Luxor. Nefertari was one of the 'Great Royal Wives' of Ramesses II, the greatest king of the 18th Dynasty.

TRAVELLER'S TIPS

Best time to go: Visit in winter or early spring (October to early April) to avoid the searing heat.

Look out for: Ensure you are well prepared for the extreme heat, and are up to date with vaccinations and inoculations.

Dos and don'ts: Do dress conservatively and behave in accordance with local customs. Do check travel restrictions in advance, as some parts of Egypt are unstable.

THE HIGH ATLAS MOUNTAINS

Start Marrakech **End** Marrakech	
Countries crossed Morocco	
Distance Trek is 160 kilometres (100 miles)	
Transport used Minivan between Marrakech and trailheads, otherwise on foot	
Highlights Marrakech, Berber villages, Jebel Toubkal, Sidi Chamarouch	

The valleys of the High Atlas Mountains are dotted with small Berber villages, whose golden brown buildings seem to have been hewn from the same material as the hills.

This journey begins in Marrakech, known as 'The Red City' for its dark, rose-coloured buildings. The 1,000-year-old city was founded by the Almoravids at the confluence of several ancient trading routes, and is still ringed by 12th-century walls with crenellated towers. The pisé walls, made of rammed earth, change hue as the sun rises and sinks, glowing pink, then red, then gold as dusk falls. However, most of this journey takes place in remote reaches of the High Atlas range and includes ascents of the highest peaks, Jebel Mgoun and Jebel Toubkal, both higher than 4,000 metres (13,000 ft).

The delicately carved minaret of the Koutoubia Mosque soars 70 metres (230 ft) above the ochre rooftops of the Marrakech medina. Built by the Almohads, who captured the city in 1147, the minaret is endowed with a special ramp that allowed the muezzin to ride to the top to lead the call to prayer. It is a beautiful structure, emulated in Seville's famous Giralda and in other towers throughout Al Andalus in Spain. The centre of city life is the Jemaa el Fna, a huge square which fills up as the day progresses with hawkers and snake charmers, dancing boys and story tellers, and later, as night falls, braziers and stalls selling vats of goat's head soup or grilled brochettes spiced with cumin and pepper. The great souk of Marrakech is a labyrinthine maze, pungent and crowded. Everything under the sun appears to be for sale, from slippers to spices and from carpets to leather. Quiet gardens provide welcome respite from the noise and bustle. In the southern section of the medina, the atmospheric ruins of the imperial palace of El Badia are spread out near the immaculately preserved 16th-century Saadian tombs, a royal mausoleum.

The Atlas Mountains are visible from any rooftop in old Marrakech, the highest peaks snowcapped for much of the year. Treks ascend through summer pastures, carpeted with wild flowers in spring, and past Berber villages, the cube-shaped homes of ochre clay arranged in terraces down the slopes. Mouflon (wild mountain sheep) and the endangered

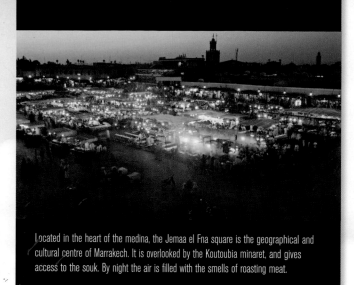

Located in the heart of the medina, the Jemaa el Fna square is the geographical and cultural centre of Marrakech. It is overlooked by the Koutoubia minaret, and gives access to the souk. By night the air is filled with the smells of roasting meat.

Cuvier gazelle inhabit the slopes, which are also remarkably rich in bird life, including the bald ibis and several raptors.

Begin the trek at Tamzrit, on the borders of the Toubkal National Park. Here tours pick up their guides and muleteers. The trail strikes west through straggling oak forest before reaching Irhil n' Ikkis, a lofty pasture with a smattering of simple huts. The following day, the ascent continues up rock-strewn slopes, with a profusion of yellow and purple broom in springtime. At the pass of Tizi n-Oumskiyk, there are tremendous views of the mighty peak of Jebel Mgoun. Camp in the shadow of the mountain before the ascent the following day. Climbing Jebel Mgoun is difficult, but fatigue is soon forgotten as you drink in the unforgettable views.

The trek continues along a green plateau, where goats and sheep graze next to a trickling stream, and then descends to the Tessaout Valley. After a night spent by the dramatic gorge of Tessaout, the trail continues past a string of steep Berber villages – Amezri, Ait Hamza and picturesque Megdaz. For the next couple of days, the route undulates dramatically, crossing verdant valleys and lofty passes. Pausing at the Kasbah of Telouet, a magical if crumbling fortress, and the lively village of Setti Fatma, famous for its waterfalls, the trail ascends once again. There are high passes to cross on successive days, the highest of which is the Tizi-n-Tacheddirt. A steep haul will bring you to the Neltner Refuge, base camp for Jebel Toubkal, at 4,167 metres (13,671 ft) the highest peak of North Africa. From the summit, a slippery climb up scree, the staggering views reach out over the mountains to the Sahara. This is the literal and figurative high point of the entire trek. Descend to Imlil, where you can be taken back to the comforts of hot showers and beds in the shimmering city of Marrakech.

All kinds of items are for sale in Marrakech's souk and bazaars, but they are most noted for their fine carpets. Be prepared for a long and elaborate haggle over cups of mint tea as you negotiate your price.

ALONG THE
SKELETON COAST

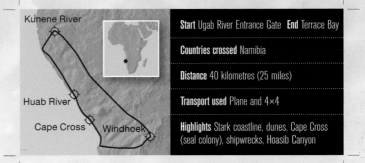

Start Ugab River Entrance Gate **End** Terrace Bay	
Countries crossed Namibia	
Distance 40 kilometres (25 miles)	
Transport used Plane and 4×4	
Highlights Stark coastline, dunes, Cape Cross (seal colony), shipwrecks, Hoasib Canyon	

The Skeleton Coast National Park encompasses one third of Namibia's Atlantic coastline, a desolate and inhospitable region of undulating dunes, fog-wreathed headlands and stark desert. The Namibian bushmen call it 'the land God made in anger', and the beaches are scattered with the wreckage of ships and the bleached bones of whales and seals. And yet, despite the extreme climate, which veers from searing heat to biting cold, the Skeleton Coast protects a surprising amount of wildlife, including rare animals such as the long-legged desert elephant, and lions that have adapted to the arid conditions. The national park remains one of the last unexplored wildernesses on Earth. The southern section can be explored along the coast road, but the northern section is a designated wilderness area and can be accessed only by fly-in safari.

The small aircraft departs from the small Namibian capital, Windhoek, and flies over the spectacular Kuiseb Canyon, which is surrounded by red dunes. As it turns over Conception Bay, you will see the dark silhouette of the *Eduard Bohlen*, the skeletal remnants of a ship which ran aground in 1909. The plane continues north over the wave-battered coastline to Cape Cross, where some 250,000 Cape fur seals congregate on the rocks, barking warnings at scavengers such as the jackals and hyena that pester the colony. If the sea fog relents, it is occasionally possible to see whales and dolphins leaping out at sea, oblivious to the treacherous currents that have led so many ships to founder on this dangerous coastline. The sea fog that wraps the beaches in dense white tentacles may be treacherous for ships, but it provides life-sustaining moisture for the plants and creatures found here. Farther north, there are aerial views of the lunar landscape of the Ugab, scarred with black craters erupting from cracked desert. These strange pockmarks are

The hull of a boat slowly rots in the corrosive sea air of the Skeleton Coast. The coast seems to stand as a metaphor for time itself: the tides and sands move in an eternal rhythm; the ships wreck and eventually become half-buried monuments.

formed by the corrosive effects of the sea salt carried on the dense fogs that creep across the coastline, and are sometimes called 'petrified ghosts'.

The plane lands near Kuidas, where camp is made near the Huab River. The following morning, depart in 4×4 vehicles to admire the curious flora and fauna that eke out a living in the harsh environment of the Huab Valley. Among the strange desert-adapted vegetation to be found here is welwitschia, with just two huge leaves often lashed to shreds by the wind, and lithops, sometimes called 'flowering stones', as well as the strange elephant's foot found in rocky crevices. Myriad species of lichen carpet the gravel plains and slopes, changing colour as they are touched by sea fog.

In the afternoon, pile into jeeps for an exploration of the mighty roaring dunes. The phenomenon is still little understood, but, as you slip down the dunes they begin to emit a low groan which crescendoes into a deep bellow. The constantly present wind whips a fine dust into the air, dancing across the endless undulations of the dunes. As dusk falls, the pale sand darkens to a deep ochre.

Take to the air once again to fly north to the next camp in the Hoarusib Valley. In the Hoarusib Canyon, the pale clay has been sculpted into a surreal landscape of storybook castles and spires, where 'waterfalls' of sand cascade magically down the canyon walls. The River Hoarusib is one of the few in this region that manages to struggle its way from the arid interior to the sea, and usually reaches the ocean at least once and sometimes twice a year.

The most northerly section of the park is part of the traditional homelands of the Himba, a nomadic people who have clung to their ancient customs and traditions despite pressure to modernize. They continue to wear goatskin clothing and stain their bodies with ochre, which represents the rich red colour of the earth, and breed cattle and goats. You may be able to visit a Himba village and learn something of their proud culture.

The plane continues north to the Kunene River on the Angolan border, a notably greener region that protects a wider variety of flora and fauna. An early morning canoe trip slips along the river, where crocodiles bask on the banks, before boarding the plane for the return flight to Windhoek.

Brown Fur Seals bask on the beach at Cape Cross, Namibia. Farther inland, birds and other animals find ways to cope with the aridity, with many getting water from the wells dug by baboons and elephants.

THE OKAVANGO DELTA

Start Maun **End** Maun	
Countries crossed Botswana	
Distance approx 200 kilometres (120 miles)	
Transport used On foot, 4x4, dugout canoe	
Highlights Spectacular scenery, game-viewing, birdwatching, rich plant life	

The Okavango is the only river on Earth to culminate in desert, flowing from the highlands of Angola into the Kalahari plains, where it fans out into a vast network of rivers, streams, lagoons and islands. This is the world's largest intact inland delta, expanding to approximately 16,000 square kilometres (6,000 sq miles) at the height of the annual floods.

The extraordinary watery landscape of the Okavango Delta is home to a staggering array of wildlife. Recent surveys have recorded 122 species of mammals, 71 species of fish, 444 species of birds and 64 species of reptiles. Among them are spectacular creatures such as lion, elephant, zebra, wildebeest, giraffe, gazelle, hippopotamus, crocodile and rhino. Although the delta is at its most luxuriant during the rainy season, the peak period for game viewing is during the dry season between May and October, when the waters shrink and the vast numbers of animals are concentrated into a smaller region. However, birders should visit during the rainy season to enjoy the widest array of birds – among them storks, kingfishers, eagles, jacana, crake, plover and goose. The delta is at its wettest when the rest of Botswana is parched and anxiously awaiting the rains: this is because the flood waters from Angola take several months to reach it.

There is very limited road access to the fringes of the delta, and most of the interior is accessible only by boat or plane. Entrance to the delta is strictly controlled, and accommodation is scarce: in effect, visitors must book a safari package. These packages usually include the plane flight into the park, accommodation and guided safaris. The comforts available depend entirely on the package chosen, with several options available in the moderate to luxury categories, but considerably fewer at the budget end.

Most flights depart from Maun, a burgeoning settlement at the southeastern tip of the delta. The aerial views from the small aircraft that convey passengers to the various lodges are astounding: the very flatness of the terrain ensures seemingly endless vistas over the huge wetlands, etched with a labyrinthine network of rivers and rivulets, islands and lagoons. Although the constantly changing course of the region's waterways means that islands appear and disappear with astonishing frequency, the Chief's Island is one of the largest and most permanent land masses in the southeast of the delta. It is among the most beautiful regions in the delta, replete with a staggering variety of plant, animal and bird life. Historically this abundance made it a particularly sought-after hunting ground, which was always claimed by the local chief – hence the name.

A herd of lechwe retreats to the relative safety of the shallow waters. The most commonly seen mammal in the Okavango Delta, gathering in herds of thousands of individuals, the lechwe has specially adapted long hind legs to allow it to run in the marshy conditions.

The Chief's Island boasts several lodges, each of which generally organizes two activities a day, one in the morning and one in the afternoon. These may take place on foot, by 4x4 or, best of all, in the traditional dugout canoes called *mokoro*, which the indigenous peoples of the region have used for centuries. Once, these small boats were painstakingly handcarved from ebony and kigelia trees, which took about a century to grow to the right size: now, locals use fibre-glass versions, but they are still poled along

the rivers in time-honoured tradition. Iridescent dragonflies flit around the boat, and water lilies unfurl in all their waxy splendour. An occasional splash provides warning of crocodiles, lurking in the reeds. The *mokoro* cruises drowsily through the water channels, stopping occasionally at islands where you can watch giraffes grazing or monkeys swinging through the trees, as huge herds of elephants and buffalo amble across the swamps. The most commonly seen creature is the lechwe, a type of antelope, which will plunge into the waters in order to escape predators. If you're lucky, you might spot its elusive little cousin, the sitatunga, which lives in the water. An estimated 200,000 large mammals are found around the delta in the dry season. This is the best time to see the great predators in action,

A pride of lionesses approaches a pond to drink. In the dry season, the area covered by the delta almost halves, and there are rich pickings for the lions as their prey is forced closer together.

as the shrinking waters oblige large numbers of animals to share resources and exist in close proximity, sparking inevitable conflicts.

For humans, the most feared creature in these parts is not the lion or the leopard, but the hippopotamus, which leaves a tell-tale trail of bubbles in the water that local guides know to avoid. Powerboats provide a less romantic but practical way to explore the waterways, and can convey travellers out to the larger lakes where hippos wallow in the shallows, and crocodiles lurk on the shores. The best way to see the larger game, including lion prides, is usually on one of the 4x4 tours, accompanied by an armed guard (the firearms are used to frighten a charging animal, and are loaded with tranquilizers).

THE GOLDEN TRIANGLE

Start Chiang Rai **End** Chiang Rai	
Countries crossed Thailand, Laos, Myanmar	
Distance 200 kilometres (125 miles)	
Transport used Bus and boat	
Highlights Chiang Rai, Mai Sai, Sop Ruak, Chiang Saen	

A lush valley in Bagan, Myanmar, is home to an extraordinary community of ancient Buddhist temples, ranging from crumbling stone stupas to glittering pagodas.

The confluence of the Ruak and Mekong Rivers forms the border between Thailand, Laos and Myanmar. Locals call the meeting of the waters 'Sop Ruak', and a small town has grown up in the environs. This frontier region was formerly the Lanna Kingdom, and is scattered with historic towns, the remnants of ancient settlements, and magnificent temples. The rugged peaks and river banks are inhabited by hill tribes, including the Karen, Hmong, Yao, Lahu, Lisu and Akha, and their traditional villages make for a fascinating introduction into local culture. The region has been growing opium since the 1920s, and remains the world's biggest heroin-producer after Afghanistan. This illicit trade is largely hidden from visitors, for whom the main attractions of the Golden Triangle are the beautiful landscapes, historic sites, varied cultures, lavish temples and serene pace of life.

Chiang Rai is the gateway to the Golden Triangle, an agreeable little city that makes the best base for touring the local attractions. Founded in 1262 by Mengrai, who established the Lanna Kingdom, it sits amid gentle hills on the banks of the River Kok. It was here that one of the most famous statues of the Buddha, the Phra Kaeo ('Emerald Buddha'), was discovered in 1432. According to legend, a bolt of lightning struck a temple stupa, which split open to reveal a magnificent

Buddha sculpted in jade. The original, still highly revered, is in Bangkok, but a copy gazes out serenely from the Wat Phra Kaeo. Visit the Night Bazaar, to rummage among stalls selling everything from silks to souvenirs, and pick up street food from the pungent food stands.

From Chiang Rai, head north towards the Thai-Myanmar border at Mai Sai. Detour east to visit the Doi Tung mountain, crowned by the ancient temple of Wat Phrathat Doi Tung, still an important Buddhist pilgrimage site. The drive winds through magnificent jungles, inhabited by several hill villages. The Princess Mother Villa, built for the present

TRAVELLER'S TIPS

Best time to go: Ideally, come from November to February, when it is dry and cool. Avoid the rainy season (June to October) if possible.

Look out for: You don't need visas to hop across the Laos or Myanmar borders, but you will need them if you intend travelling farther.

Dos and don'ts: Do haggle for bargains; it is expected and part of the local culture.

The golden dome of the Dhamma Ya Zi Ka Pagoda in Myanmar is one of thousands of pagodas in the country, often known as the 'Land of Pagodas'. Myanmar has more monks per head of population than any other country where Buddhism is practised. In recent times they have led popular protests against the country's military rulers.

Thai king's late mother, is surrounded by exquisite gardens and is now a museum. Mai Sai straddles the frontier with Myanmar, a burgeoning tourist town full of stalls selling typical Burmese crafts, including brightly coloured textiles and sculpted jade. You can cross the border to find another market town, Tha Khi Lek, just inside Myanmar itself.

Head southeast to Sop Ruak, the epicentre of the Golden Triangle, where the confluence of the Ruak and Mekong rivers forms the border between three countries. A small settlement has grown up by the water's edge, with a slew of cafés and souvenir shops, and a pair of museums that describe the development of the opium trade in the region. The 1,200-year-old temple of Wat Phrathat Phu Khao occupies a small hill just outside the town, with a lookout point offering excellent views over the three countries.

From Sop Ruak, pick up a boat for the 40-minute cruise down the Mekong to Chiang Saen, once one of the most important cities in the Lanna Kingdom. Although most of the city was razed in 1804 by the Siamese King in order to prevent further Burmese incursions, it still retains remnants of the original late 13th- and early 14th-century monuments erected under King Saen Phu. These include parts of the ancient earthern ramparts which enfolded the city on three sides, with the Mekong providing a natural barrier to the east. The National Museum offers a good introduction to Chiang Saen's colourful history. Within the old city walls, there are several exquisite temples,

Children head home along the River Mekong near Luang Prabang in Laos. Despite its tranquil appearance, the river is not easy to navigate – it experiences a seasonal variation in flow and there are frequent rapids.

including the Wat Phra That Chedi Luang, which is studded with the largest *chedi* (stupa) in the city, and was built in 1489. Lost amid extensive teak forest on the fringes of Chiang Saen is the Wat Pa Sak, constructed in 1295 by Saen Phu, with a magnificent *chedi* and intricate decoration. Return to Chiang Rai, where the journey ends.

A TROPICAL PARADISE

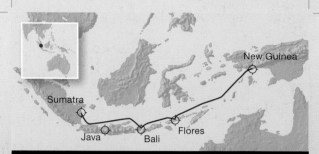

Indonesia is an archipelago nation that comprises more than 17,000 islands, incorporating a diverse range of cultures and landscapes. While the cities and resorts hum with life and excitement, the smaller islands provide respite from the crowds with perfect tropical beaches and a teeming underwater world around the multi-coloured reefs. The islands are linked by a network of ferries.

Sumatra is one of the largest islands in the world, with the vast mountains of Bukit Barisan stretching along its western coast. The northern part of the island is a paradise for nature-lovers, with prolific wildlife in the remote rainforest and jagged peaks. The Gunung Leuser Park occupies almost

8,000 square kilometres (3,000 sq miles) of pristine mountains, and is one of the last two surviving habitats of the Sumatran orangutan. It also shelters the endangered Sumatran tiger and Sumatran rhinoceros. Mount Kerinci, the highest volcano in Indonesia, is the centrepiece of the Kerinci Sablat National Park.

Java, the next island in the chain, is home to the Indonesian capital, Jakarta. The city embodies the country's booming economy, the benefits of which have yet to reach the poor, and glossy new skyscrapers stand cheek-by-jowl with shanty towns. Sleepier Malang, with its faded colonial buildings and colourful markets, makes a more attractive base. At the centre of the island is the world's largest Buddhist monument, Borobudur. This huge pyramid was built in about 750 AD

in the middle of a plain overlooked by the active volcano Mount Merapi. It is constructed in the form of a mandala, a physical representation of Buddhist cosmology, and the path up the pyramid to its summit represents the journey towards nirvana. Each level is decorated with intricately sculpted reliefs depicting events in the life of the Buddha.

The party island of Bali is next, its gorgeous white beaches, cobalt blue waters and giddy nightlife a magnet for holiday-makers from around the world. But away from the hubbub of the coast lie tranquil villages where life continues at a relaxed pace. Kintamini is a delightful base, with fine hikes to the shimmering Batur Lake and superb views of the active volcano Gunung Batur. Lovina on the north coast is a laid-back resort that offers dolphin-watching trips.

The Ulun Danu Temple is a floating Hindu temple at Candi Kunung on the shores of Lake Bratan in Bali. Most Indonesians are Muslim, but there are significant minorities of Hindus, Buddhists and Christians.

Farmers in Bali still cultivate their coconut trees by hand, climbing the long trunks without the use of harnesses. Terraced fields allow them to grow crops such as rice on the mountainous island.

The temple of Tanah Lot, just west of Denpasar, is a spectacular sight, perched on a volcanic outcrop. Lombok, east of Bali, is similarly scattered with resorts and fabulous beaches, but is considerably quieter than its sister. The larger resorts, along with the best surfing beaches, are in the south, but the north of the island remains stunningly wild and unspoilt. The tiny trio of the Gili Islands are world-renowned for the diving and snorkelling opportunities afforded around the magnificent reefs. No vehicles are allowed here, and donkey-drawn carts are the main form of transport.

The island of Flores is scattered with bamboo villages and verdant rice paddies. The enormous volcano of Mount Kelimatu is an easy climb, and offers tremendous views of three glimmering lakes. The islands of Komodo and Rinca are part of a protected nature reserve, with a surreal, rocky landscape where the huge lizard, the Komodo dragon, thrives.

Finally, the journey culminates in New Guinea, the world's second largest island; the western portion belongs to Indonesia, while the eastern half is an independent nation. The island is home to between five and ten per cent of the total species of flora and fauna on the planet, many of which have still to be documented. Culturally, it is equally rich, with approximately 1,000 tribal groupings, along with a rich ethnic diversity bequeathed by waves of settlers. The island is dominated by huge peaks, rising to almost 5,000 metres (16,000 ft). Much of the pristine coastline and its superb coral reefs is protected, providing unparalleled opportunities for glimpsing myriad marine creatures.

A dominant male orangutan surveys his kingdom in the forests of northern Sumatra. These great apes are the largest tree-dwelling animals in the world, and males may weigh up to 90 kilogrammes (200 lb). Fewer than 10,000 Sumatran orangutans remain in the wild. They are only found here and on the neighbouring island of Borneo.

Lying in the Coral Sea just off the coast of Queensland, the Great Barrier Reef is the world's largest reef system, comprising 2,900 individual reefs and 900 islands.

TRAVELLER'S TIPS

Best time to go: The tracks are only passable in the dry season, between April and November.

Look out for: Ensure your vehicle is equipped with the required recovery gear. Some communities have a ban on alcohol, and will impose heavy fines if the laws are broken.

Dos and don'ts: Do be respectful of Aboriginal community laws. Do check road conditions before making the journey.

The Daintree Rainforest National Park lies to the north of Cairns. This unspoilt rainforest is an important area of research and scientists use 50-metre (165-ft) cranes to reach and study wildlife in the canopy.

CAPE YORK

Start Cairns **End** Thursday Island	
Countries crossed Australia	
Distance 1,500 kilometres (930 miles)	
Transport used 4x4, ferry	
Highlights Cairns, Daintree Rainforest National Park, Cooktown, Aboriginal rock art sites around Laura, the Old Telegraph Track, the tip of Australia, Torres Strait Islands	

Cairns is gloriously set on Queensland's eastern coast, surrounded by rainforest and boasting a magnificent coastline etched with beaches and bays. It is the main gateway for the celebrated Great Barrier Reef, the world's largest reef system. To the north of the city, the Daintree Rainforest National Park protects one of the oldest ecosystems on Earth, and the towering tree canopy is home to a vast number of plant and animal species.

The route north from Cairns towards Cooktown follows an unsealed track suitable only for four-wheel-drive vehicles. Along the way, mountains clad in rainforest spill down to the shore, and the track crosses streams and craggy bays, past sweeping beaches, headlands and islets. Cooktown is named after Captain James Cook, who landed here in 1770, and is a charming, low-key harbour town on the shores of the Endeavour River. The Mount Cook, Endeavour and Black Mountain National Parks are on the doorstep, and the excellent fishing is complemented by superb hiking trails. To the east lies the small settlement of Laura, which has been home to Aboriginal communities for 50,000 years and is surrounded by prehistoric Aboriginal rock art sites.

The route north continues along unsealed tracks, winding its way through pristine rainforest, past old mining towns, telegraph stations, swamps and lagoons and across several dramatic river crossings. Beyond the Jardine River, a magnificent coastal landscape unfolds with stunning beaches, particularly at Umagico, Loyalty Beach and Seisia. From Pajinka, a short trek leads to a rocky outcrop where a sign proclaims 'You are now standing at the end of the Australian continent'. Ferries heading north link the peninsula with Thursday Island, the main centre of the Torres Strait Islands, which is blessed with stunning beaches and bays.

THE GREAT OCEAN ROAD

Start Geelong **End** Port Fairy

Countries crossed Australia

Distance 250 kilometres (150 miles) **Transport used** Car

Highlights Geelong, Torquay, Great Otway National Park, the Twelve Apostles, Port Fairy

The Great Ocean Road stretches along the breathtaking coast of Victoria in Southern Australia, passing historic villages and quiet rivers, rugged cliffs and emerald bays. This is one of the world's greatest surfing destinations, but there are plenty of other activities on offer, from horse-riding to golf.

The starting point, Geelong, is a large city on the Barwon River overlooking an expansive bay. There are numerous opportunities here for sailing, surfing and other watersports. Vineyards spread across the hills around Geelong, and several wineries are open for visits. To the south is Torquay, a relaxed town world-famous for its surfing beaches. This rugged stretch of coastline, with its towering cliffs and bluffs, boasts several spectacular strands, some of which are suitable for families, while others will test the skills of even the most experienced surfers. Scenic trails unfurl along the cliffs.

West of Torquay, the little resort of Anglesey boasts more beautiful beaches, and a quiet, small-town atmosphere. Fishing, horse-riding and canoeing are among the activities on offer. At the hamlet of Aireys Inlet, the Split Point lighthouse, built in the 19th century and still functioning, can be toured and offers mesmerizing views over the coastline from the top.

The drive hugs the coastline as it wends south towards Lorne, a tranquil village tucked around a sheltered bay. Its rocky shores are good for snorkelling and diving. Green hills spill down to the coast, and the fishing, particularly along the Erskine River, is excellent. Kennett River is one of the best places in Australia to see koalas in the wild. They spend most of the day resting in the gum trees, but begin to forage and move around in the late afternoon.

Farther west, Apollo Bay is another charming resort huddled around a fishing harbour. It is the gateway to the Great Otway National Park, a pristine wilderness with some of the most beautiful waterfalls in the entire country. These include the Hopetoun Falls, the Erskine Falls and the stunning Triplet Falls, with a trio of cascading streams. From there, the road zigzags over Cape Otway, with forest and hills stretching out on either side, and glorious views extending over the jagged coast. As the route dips towards Port Campbell, it offers stunning views of the Twelve Apostles, a cluster of rocky stacks

Misleadingly, the Twelve Apostles was the name given to a group of nine limestone stacks eroded from the cliff face in Port Campbell National Park. In 2005 one of the stacks collapsed, so now only eight remain.

The eastern grey kangaroo is the most commonly seen kangaroo in Australia. This adaptable marsupial is often found very close to built-up areas. You are most likely to spot one in the early morning or evening, as they shelter from the sun in woodlands during the day.

jutting up from the turquoise waters. These have become one of the most famous landmarks in Australia, and the whole area is protected in the Port Campbell National Park, a dedicated marine reserve. Sightseeing boats that ply the coast give close-up views of the rocky bridges and arches. This wild, wave-lashed coastline has proved treacherous for mariners, and is still sometimes called 'Shipwreck Coast'. Beyond the hamlet of Peterborough, more lofty stacks protrude dramatically from the foaming sea. The Bay of Islands is hauntingly lovely, and attracts considerably fewer visitors than the Twelve Apostles.

The road dips inland as it approaches the western end of the Great Ocean Road and the tranquil town of Warrnambool. There are long, family-friendly beaches here, spectacular coves and headlands to explore, and a range of activities from diving to hiking. The Mahogany Walking Track meanders along deserted beaches all the way to Port Fairy. If you visit between June and October, head to Logan's Beach, an important breeding ground for the southern right whale.

There are several more opportunities for wildlife watching west of Warrnambool, including the Tower Hill Stage Game Reserve, beautifully set inside the cone of an extinct volcano. There are seal colonies at Port Fairy, an enchanting fishing village that has preserved many of its original buildings from the 19th century. A wonderful walk cuts through petrified forest to the tip of Cape Bridgewater where fur seals cluster on the rocks, or you can take boats out to Lady Julia Percy Island. Blue whales spend the summers (November to March) feeding on krill off the coast west of Port Fairy, when whale-watching tours are offered from nearby Portland.

The idyllic Hopetoun Falls, near Apollo Bay on the Great Ocean Road, plunge 30 metres (100 ft) into a tropical river. They are a popular visitor attraction along the route.

TRAVELLER'S TIPS

Best time to go: This journey is wonderful at any time of the year. Come in summer to enjoy the beaches, or in winter to escape the crowds and go hiking or wildlife watching. Avoid the busy period from late December to end January.

Look out for: The Great Ocean Road is a single lane road in each direction, often steep, with blind hairpin bends.

Dos and don'ts: Do visit wineries, dairies and markets to try the local produce.

NORTH ISLAND

Cape Reinga
Bay Of Islands
Waipoua Forest
Auckland
Tauranga
Rotorua
Lake Taupo
Tongariro
Napier
Hastings
Martinborough
Wellington

Start Wellington **End** Cape Reinga

Countries crossed New Zealand

Distance 1,000 kilometres (600 miles)

Transport used Car

Highlights Wellington, wine regions, Lake Taupo, Tongariro National Park, Rotorua, Coromandel Peninsula, Auckland, Waipoua Forest, Bay of Islands

This route travels up the spine of New Zealand's North Island from the city of Wellington all the way to its northernmost tip. On the way, it passes volcanoes and vines, lakes and hot springs, vast forests and dazzling bays. These thrilling landscapes have formed the backdrop to countless films, most famously the *Lord of the Rings* trilogy.

Begin in Wellington, a vibrant and charming city draped over a series of volcanic ridges and valleys, with gabled houses painted in ice-cream colours. It is surrounded by forested valleys and overlooks a vast bay where the Pacific and Southern oceans meet. The Te Panu National Museum is excellent, but the city is also full of great galleries, museums and arty cafés.

From Wellington, a fast motorway whizzes through the verdant Hutt Valley before climbing over the Rimutaka Range towards Martinborough. The gentle hills are traced with endless fields of vines, and the environs of this charming town are dotted with boutique wineries which can be visited for tours and tastings. Continue east to Hastings on Hawke's Bay to explore the largest wine-producing region on the North Island. These fertile lands have long produced an abundance of fruit and vegetables, but now the area is increasingly well known for its delicious red wines. Just north of Hastings, Napier is a large seaport, with a host of glamorous Art Deco buildings. It's become a popular resort, and its restaurants are celebrated for their fine cuisine.

Turn west from Napier into the mountainous hinterland to reach Lake Taupo, New Zealand's largest lake, which is cradled in a vast volcanic crater. The volcano last erupted in 181 AD, jetting forth columns of ash and lava with such force that the skies turned scarlet as far afield as Rome and China. The geothermal activity now bubbles underground, surfacing in the natural hot springs and mud pools for which the lake is famous. This is a spectacular destination for a host of activities, including fishing, bungee-jumping, sailing, hiking and whitewater rafting. The spectacular Huka Falls drain out of Lake Taupo, the waters funnelled through a natural canyon before plunging powerfully over the clifftop. The lake is overlooked by three volcanoes – Tongariro, Ruapehu and Ngauruhoe – forming the heart of the Tongariro National Park, which protects an area sacred to Maori. Maori legend holds that these mighty peaks were once gods and warriors, who battled for the attentions of the goddess Pihanga. Tongariro was the victor. Today, the volcano's slopes offer superb hiking, including the Tongariro Crossing, an intense one-day hike to a cobalt-blue lake high above the clouds.

Continue northeast to reach Rotorua, sprawled along the shores of another geothermal lake, where steaming hot springs and bubbling mud pools are found on the river banks, and

Mount Ruapehu, in the Tongariro National Park, is one of the most active volcanoes in the world. At 2,797 metres (9,177 ft), it is the highest point on North Island. Its frequent volcanic activity has created a deep crater, which fills with a lake between major eruptions.

TRAVELLER'S TIPS

Best time to go: Peak season is December to January, so visit October to Christmas or February to April to avoid the crowds. For skiing, visit in July to August.

Look out for: Film buffs can seek out the locations for the *Lord of the Rings* trilogy, as well as the *Narnia* films also shot on the North Island.

Dos and don'ts: Do try to time your visit with local festivals, such as Napier's food festival or the jazz festival in the Bay of Islands.

Urupukapuka is the largest island in the Bay of Islands, a 16-kilometre (10-mile)-wide inlet on the northeast coast of North Island. The bay is a popular destination for sailors and big-game fishing.

geysers – most famously, the Pohutu Geyser at Whakarewarewa – jet powerfully from the ground. From Roturua, head north to Tauranga and follow the road around the beautiful Bay of Plenty to arrive at Thames, gateway to the magnificent Coromandel Peninsula. Although it is squeezed by the big cities of Tauranga and Auckland, the peninsula's rugged terrain has kept development to a minimum. Much of this region is thickly covered in dense rainforest, and the coastline boasts dazzling white sand beaches. Over the last few decades, the peninsula has increasingly attracted people looking for an alternative, environmentally friendly lifestyle, and the towns and the resorts are laid-back and friendly.

Heading northwest, Auckland is a large modern city straddling a narrow peninsula and overlooking a vast natural harbour. Continue beyond Whangarei to the Bay of Islands, where the electric blue sea is scattered with some 150 islands, and the coastline is etched with rivers and waterfalls. Hiking, diving, sailing, birdwatching or simply relaxing on the perfect white sand beaches are just some of the many activities on offer.

Inland from the Bay of Islands stretches the Waipoua Forest, which protects one of the last swathes of virgin woodland on the North Island, particularly the enormous Kairi, one of the world's mightiest trees. The showpiece of the forest is the Tane Mahuta, a 2,000-year-old giant with a trunk 14 metres (45 ft) in circumference. A variety of trails suitable for hikers of all levels are traced through the serene forest.

Finally, you reach the very tip of New Zealand, Cape Reinga. According to the Maori tradition, it is from this finger of land that the spirits of the departed leap to make their final journey to their ancestral home of Hawaiki. The headland is covered in dense forest where wild horses roam.

This vineyard near Napier is in the heart of the North Island's main wine-making region, Hawke's Bay, whose long, hot summers and cool winters provide the perfect climate for growing grapes. The region is particularly renowned for its red wines, especially the Bordeaux and Syrah varieties.

THE MILFORD TRACK

The Milford Track strikes through the magnificent mountains, forests and wetlands of the Fiordland National Park on New Zealand's South Island. The four-day 'tramp' is often called 'The Finest Walk in the World', after an article published in 1908 by poet Blanche Baughan, and has its roots in a Maori trail used for transporting valuable greenstone (a type of jade). The Maoris call this swathe of the southern island Te Wahipounamu, meaning 'place of the greenstone', which has been inscribed on UNESCO's World Heritage List for its astonishing beauty, cultural importance and abundance of endemic flora and fauna.

The Milford Track was first discovered by European explorers in the 19th century, and has become one of the country's premier hikes. The trail culminates in Milford Sound, a deep, mirror-like fjord gouged into sheer mountains. According to Maori legend, the god Tu-te-raki-whanoa was given the task of carving out this coastline, each bay emerging more lovelier than the next, until he surpassed himself with the sublime beauty of Milford Sound. Another tale relates that the Maori goddess Hinenui-te-Po released swarms of sandflies into Milford Sound so that humans would not linger in such an enchanting place. Sandflies remain a scourge, and savvy travellers come well prepared with protective clothing.

Each year about 14,000 people walk the Milford Track, which is tightly regulated to minimize the impact of visitors. Only 90 people can begin the trail each day (40 independent walkers, and 50 guided walkers), all of whom are required to stay at the huts provided by the Department of Conservation. This means that the trail must be walked in the same direction (north to south) and that hikers are required to keep walking, even if weather conditions deteriorate, in order to reach the next night's accommodation.

Milford Sound is surrounded by sheer rock faces that rise over 1,200 metres (3,900 ft). The area is one of the wettest in New Zealand, and heavy rain creates dozens of temporary waterfalls.

Sutherland Falls cascades 580 metres (1,900 ft) from Lake Quill at the top to form the Arthur River at the bottom. The falls are so high that the water passes through several distinct climate zones as it descends, from alpine meadows around the lake to temperate rainforest at the bottom.

The trail begins at Glade Wharf on Lake Te Anau, a vast, serene lake surrounded by snow-capped peaks. It is the second-largest body of fresh water by surface area in New Zealand, with three dramatic fjords gouged into its western shores. Te Anau means 'cave of the swirling water' in Maori, the name inspired by a subterranean cave system gouged out by rushing rivers. The caves are a popular local sight, eerily illuminated by the green-blue light emanating from thousands of glow worms. From the shores of Lake Te Anau, the trail follows the Clinton River, passing through beech forest and offering occasional glimpses of the mountain passes that await.

On the second day, hikers ascend the valley, passing numerous lakes and waterfalls, including Hidden Lake, with its sheer rock walls and wispy waterfalls, and Prairie Lake, which offers superb views back over the valley and is good for a dip if the sun is shining. As the route ascends, beech gives way to ribbonwood, before culminating at Mintaro Hut, where independent hikers spend the second night.

The third day of the track is the most thrilling, with exhilarating views over valley and peaks from the famous Mackinnon Pass (1,073 metres/3,520 ft). The pass is named after the pioneer explorer and surveyor Quintin Mackinnon, a charismatic figure who became the first guide on the track. The descent follows the Roaring Burn, a rapid stream cascading beautifully in a series of rapids and waterfalls. A short side-trip will bring you to the

Sutherland Falls, the fifth highest waterfall in the world. The cascading waters are whipped into fine mist by the wind.

There are more beautiful waterfalls to seek out on the final day's hike, including the Mackay Falls, which plummets gracefully over mossy boulders. The route continues past Lake Ada and the powerful Giant Gate Falls to the terminus at Sandfly Point. There is no road access from this remote spot, but ferries run regularly to the coast, gliding across Milford Sound, where silent mountains stand sentinel over glassy waters.

The Milford Track starts at the northern tip of Lake Te Anau, which is the largest freshwater lake by volume in Australasia, with a maximum depth of 417 metres (1,368 ft).

THE SAIGON-HANOI EXPRESS

Start Hanoi **End** Ho Chi Minh City	
Countries crossed Vietnam	
Distance 1,760 kilometres (1,090 miles)	
Transport used Train	
Highlights Hanoi, Ninh Binh, Hué, Da Nang, Nha Trang, Ho Chi Minh City	

The Vietnamese describe their country as 'two rice baskets on either end of a carrying pole'. The 'rice basket' of the north is Hanoi, the historic capital, with temples and pagodas reflected in shimmering lakes. To the south is Ho Chi Minh City, formerly known as Saigon, which is chaotic and vibrant, with markets, beaches and faded French colonial architecture. The cities are linked by the Reunification Express, a railway that cuts through the spine of the country, past rice paddies and mist-covered hills.

Hanoi sits on the banks of the Red River, its temples and pagodas a graceful reminder of its ancient history. At the heart of the city is the Old Quarter, a cluster of narrow streets still named after the goods made and sold here for centuries – Silk Street, Tinsmith Street, Coffin Street.

The first stop on the train is Ninh Binh. This peaceful country town is set amid verdant hills, the countryside etched with rice paddies still ploughed by water buffalo. Heading south, Da Nang is a busy seaport and a good base for exploring remarkable sights, such as the ancient My Son Hindu temple complex or the preserved port of Hoi An, where wooden-hulled boats still bob in the harbour. The next station stop is Nha Trang, Vietnam's most famous seaside resort, where white-sand beaches, an emerald sea and beautiful mountains inset with waterfalls make this the perfect place to linger.

The southern terminus is Ho Chi Minh City, where the scars of the conflict that ripped the country apart from 1955 to 1975 are still evident in the War Remnants Museum and Reunification Palace. Head to the Ben Tanh market to slurp down noodles and gaze at the piles of silks, before relaxing on the white-sand beaches just outside the city.

Beyond the Old Quarter stretches the tranquil expanse of the Hoan Kiem Lake, 'Lake of the Restored Sword', which legend relates is where a fisherman found the sacred sword used to vanquish the Chinese invaders.

Citizens of Hanoi take early morning exercise along Ho Van Park Lake. Built on lowland between rivers, Hanoi has many scenic lakes, and is sometimes known as the 'city of lakes'.

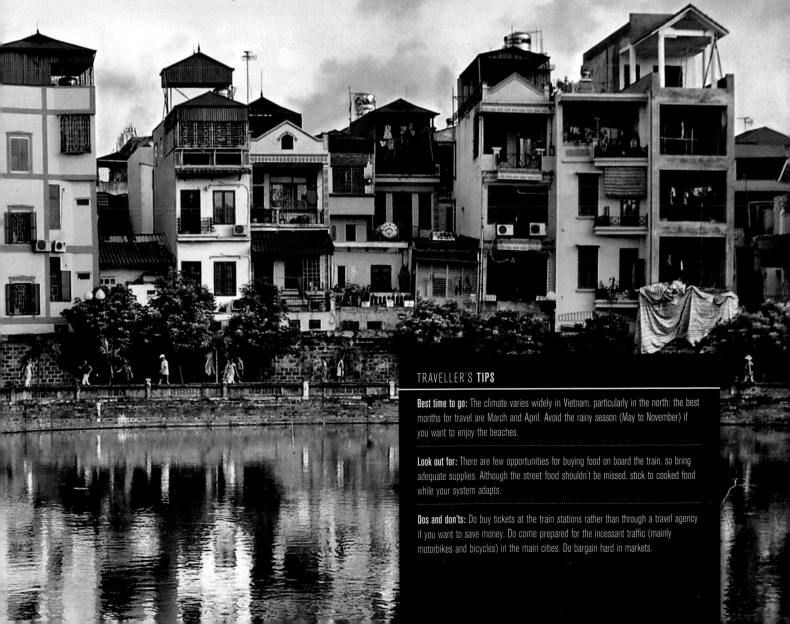

TRAVELLER'S TIPS

Best time to go: The climate varies widely in Vietnam, particularly in the north: the best months for travel are March and April. Avoid the rainy season (May to November) if you want to enjoy the beaches.

Look out for: There are few opportunities for buying food on board the train, so bring adequate supplies. Although the street food shouldn't be missed, stick to cooked food while your system adapts.

Dos and don'ts: Do buy tickets at the train stations rather than through a travel agency if you want to save money. Do come prepared for the incessant traffic (mainly motorbikes and bicycles) in the main cities. Do bargain hard in markets.

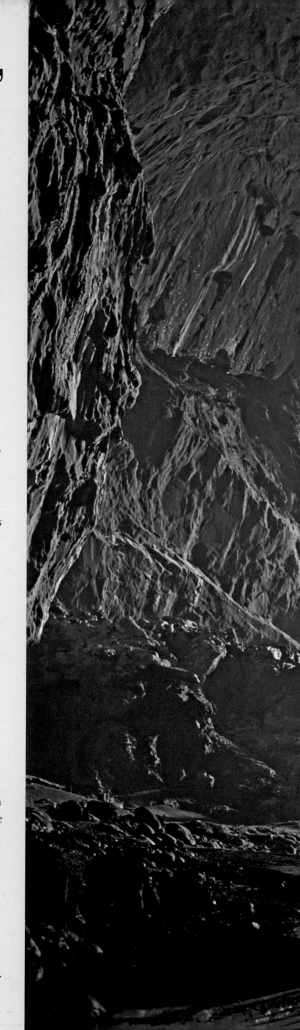

THE HEADHUNTERS' TRAIL

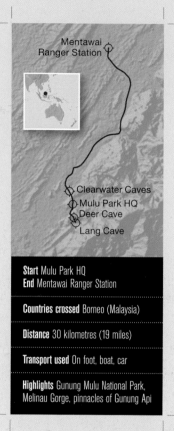

Start Mulu Park HQ
End Mentawai Ranger Station

Countries crossed Borneo (Malaysia)

Distance 30 kilometres (19 miles)

Transport used On foot, boat, car

Highlights Gunung Mulu National Park, Melinau Gorge, pinnacles of Gunung Api

Much of the island of Borneo is covered by towering mountains and rainforest. The route through the remote jungle and rivers of the Gunung Mulu National Park in Sarawak, eastern Borneo, follows ancient trails and explores the largest and most spectacular cave systems on Earth. Travellers also have the opportunity to stay in a traditional longhouse built by the indigenous Iban peoples. These enormous traditional dwellings are built on stilts and usually accommodate an entire village.

The journey begins with a short trek to Deer Cave and Lang Cave, part of the world's largest cave system. At dusk, millions of bats fly out of the caves and up into the sky to search for food. The journey north continues in a long-tail boat, a slender wooden craft, which is navigated along the tea-coloured waters to the settlement of Batu Bungan, where local Penan people offer their traditional crafts for sale. The boat journey leads to the Wind Cave, with a forest of delicate stalagmites, and the Clearwater Caves, which overlook a natural swimming pool shaded with giant trees.

Towering above the forest is the huge sandstone crag of Gunung Mulu, which gives the park its name. The crag can be climbed, but some of the harder parts involve navigating ladders and ropes. However, the sight of the pale stone pinnacles rising like spires through the forest is worth the effort.

The Headhunters' Trail then leads to the banks of the River Terikan. The trek gets its name from the Kayan war parties who paddled up the River Baram, then dragged their canoes across the forest to the Terikan in order to attack the people of the Limbang Valley. The heads of their enemies were brought back as prizes. This section of the trek is especially rich in wildlife, including giant porcupines.

Another long-tail boat awaits at the river, and will bring you to an Iban settlement where you spend the night in a longhouse. You may be greeted by the chief, and perhaps be offered a cup of *tuak*, local rice wine. The people are friendly and visitors may be invited to join in with traditional dancing or to try their hand at fishing according to centuries-old practices. The next day, a boat takes visitors to Nanga Mendamit, where 4x4s await for the transfer to Limbang.

The vast entrance to Deer Cave leads into
a massive system of caves that stretches
more than 4 kilometres (2.5 miles)
underground and links up with Lang Cave.

TRAVELLER'S **TIPS**

Best time to go: Avoid the rainy season between November and February.

Look out for: Be sensitive to cultural differences when staying with the Ibans.
Bring insect repellant.

Dos and don'ts: Do pack lightly. Do be prepared for the trek, which is
physically challenging.

INDEX

ACKNOWLEDGEMENTS

Quercus Publishing Plc
55 Baker Street
7th Floor, South Block
London
W1U 8EW

First published in 2012
Copyright © Quercus Publishing 2012

Text by Mary-Ann Gallagher

Every effort has been made to contact copyright holders. However, the publishers will be glad to rectify in future editions any inadvertent omissions brought to their attention.

A catalogue record of this book is available from the British Library.

UK and associated territories:
ISBN 978 1 78087 157 8

Printed and bound in China

10 9 8 7 6 5 4 3 2 1

Created for Quercus by Tall Tree Books Ltd

Managing editor: David John
Designers: Ed Simkins, Jonathan Vipond
Indexer: Christine Bernstein

Picture Credits

GI = Getty Images

tl = top left
bl = bottom left
tr = top right
br = bottom right

2–3 Guy Vanderelst/GI; 8–9 Jami Tarris/GI; 9br Norbert Wu/GI; 10–11 Guy Edwardes/GI; 12–13 Rough Guides/Paul Whitfield/GI; 14–15 David Muench/GI; 16–17 Carr Clifton/GI; 17tr Harald Sund/GI; 18–19 Michio Hoshino/GI; 20–21 Richard Price/GI; 22tl Noel Kleinman/GI; 22–23 Don Smith/GI, 24–25 Bob Stefko/GI, 26–27 Noel Hendrickson/GI, 26bl Design Pics/Richard Wear/GI; 28–29 Adam Jones/GI; 30–31 Wilbur E. Garrett/GI; 32–33 Keren Su/GI; 33 Robert Frerck/GI, 34–35 83213437/ Claude Bouchard, 36–37 Piotr Naskrecki/GI, 38–39 Patrick Di Fruscia/Visuals Unlimited/GI; 39tr Marco Simoni/GI; 40–41 David Sutherland/GI; 42–43 Sylvain Sonnet/GI; 43br Doug Armand/GI; 44–45 Marcus Lyon/GI; 45 Kevin Schafer/GI, 46–47 David Tipling/GI; 48–49 Danita Delimont/GI; 50–51 Frans Lemmens/GI, 52tl Getty Images, 52–53 David Madison/GI; 54–55 Konrad Wothe/GI, 56–57 Art Wolfe/GI, 56bl Don Klumpp/GI; 58–59 Visions Of Our Land/GI; 60–61 Stuart Dee/GI, 62–63 Simeone Huber/GI, 64–65 Andrea Pistolesi/GI; 65br Christian Kober/GI; 66–67 Brian Lawrence/GI; 68 Paul Souders/GI; 68–69 Brian Lawrence/GI; 70–71 David Hughes/GI; 72–73 Samuel Magal/GI; 72tl Louis–Marie Preau/GI; 74–75 Gavin Hellier/GI; 76–77 altrendo travel/GI; 78–79 Jean–Pierre Pieuchot/GI; 79br Buena Vista Images/GI, 80–81 Matteo Colombo/GI, 82–83 Camille Moirenc/GI, 84–85 Design Pics/Gareth McCormack/GI; 86–87 Design Pics/Peter McCabe/GI; 87tr IIC/Axiom/GI; 88–89 Daryl Benson/GI; 90–91 Travel Ink/GI; 91 Vincenzo Lombardo/GI; 92–93 Jean–Pierre Pieuchot/GI; 94–95 Thorsten Klapsch/GI; 95br Pierre Jacques/GI; 96–97 Brigitte Merz/GI; 98–99 Silvia Otte/GI; 98 Heinz Wohner/GI; 100–101 Bjarki Reyr/GI; 102–103 Tuul/hemis.fr/GI; 103tr Steve Allen/GI; 104–105 Frank Chmura/GI; 106bl Bob van Ooik/GI; 106–107 Konrad Wothe/GI; 108–109 John and Tina Reid/GI; 109br Slow Images/GI; 110–111 Bruno Barbier/GI; 112–113 Brian Lawrence/GI; 114–115 Mats Silvan/GI; 116–117 Panoramic Images/GI; 118tl Mark Mawson/GI; 118–119 Brian Lawrence/GI; 120–121 B Holland/GI; 122tl Grant Faint/GI; 122–123 Panoramic Images/GI; 124–125 Michio Hoshino/GI; 126–127 Harald Sund/GI; 128–129 Carol Adam/GI; 129br Martin Harvey/GI; 130–131 BOISVIEUX Christophe/hemis.fr/GI; 132–133 Martin Child/GI; 134–135 Poras Chaudhary/GI; 135br Steve Allen/GI; 136–137 Yoshinori Takahashi/GI; 137br Time & Life Pictures/GI; 138–139 Roger de la Harpe/GI; 140–141 Nigel Dennis/GI; 141tr Roger de la Harpe/GI; 142–143 Thomas Dressler/GI; 144–145 Christopher Scott/GI; 146–147 Daryl Balfour/GI; 148–149 Shanna Baker/GI; 150–151 Juergen Ritterbach/GI; 151bl DEA/M. SEEMULLER/GI; 152–153 ESCUDERO Patrick/hemis.fr/GI; 154tl Kelly Cheng Travel Photography/GI; 154–155 Danita Delimont/GI; 156–157 Paul Souders/GI; 158–159 Juergen Ritterbach/GI; 160–161 Daryl Balfour/GI; 162–163 Tier Images/GI; 164–165 Stefano Politi Markovina/GI; 166bl Juergen Ritterbach/GI; 166–167 Stephen Zeigler/GI; 168–169 Otto Stadler/GI; 170bl Suzi Eszterhas/GI; 170–171 Martin Puddy/GI; 172–173 Getty Images; 172tl Chantal Ferraro/GI; 174–175 Carol Adam/GI; 176tl Theo Allofs/GI; 176–177 Slow Images/GI; 178–179 David H. Collier/GI; 180–181 Martin Ruegner/GI; 181br Frans Lemmens/GI; 182–183 travellinglight/GI; 184tl Paul Chesley/GI; 184–185 Rich Reid/GI; 186–187 Bruno De Hogues/GI; 188–189 Richard Ashworth/GI.